A Healthy Recipe for a
Balanced Life

By **DONNA FATIGATO**, C.P.T.,

Holistic Nutrition Coach

Table of Contents

If you can see it, you can do it! I have visualized this book for many years and felt in my body and mind that the finished project would be rewarding, impactful and satisfying. Regardless of how many books I sell, I have completed my vision by creating a message of hope, healing and transformation – and that to me is the most rewarding task.

I would like to dedicate this book to my clients and all of those that inspired me along the way – including a very special thanks to my wonderful husband, John, of thirty-three years who has provided me with love, laughter, support and confidence; my amazing adult children, Dominic, Erica and Sam, and my loving mother, Joann. Their love and support have been unconditional and the make-up of whom I am today.

> ### *"A goal without action is just a dream."*
>
> -Dave Ramsey

Introduction

During my life journey and wellness profession, I have tried different approaches to help people recognize their habits. These habits may have inhibited them to reach their goals, so I have encouraged them to take steps to make changes in order for them to live a better quality of life. I have come to the conclusion that you truly have to want to change. Preparation is the key to change and ultimately to achieve your goals. Preparation begins in the mind. Action follows – without action, your goal is just a dream. What is your why? Your goals? Your obstacles? The quality of life that YOU want to live? These are all questions that we are going to explore, and along the way, find solutions through inspirational client stories, awareness of YOUR life goal and purpose, finding balance in your life and a diet-free approach to a healthy, quality life.

Some people succumb to their genetic background. Applying the holistic approaches throughout this book, however, can help you live a better quality of life. Can you change your genetic pathway? I realized during my teenage years, around 17 years of age, that my habits and genetic pipeline needed to be altered. This is a rare revelation from someone that young, but my frequent visits to the local fast-food chain found me ordering a burger, fries and a chocolate shake – and, of course,

I super-sized it. I suffered from digestive issues and Raynaud's disease, an autoimmune condition which stopped me from actively participating in the sports and activities that I so enjoyed. At the home front, my dad would be idle on the couch suffering from rheumatoid arthritis. His previously active life was no longer filled with the activities that he once enjoyed. The history of cancer and life-threatening diseases was strong in both my mom's and dad's side of the family. My dad died young, at the age of 61, and battled crippling arthritis, emphysema and Hodgkin's lymphoma during his lifetime. My mom was diagnosed with pancreatic cancer when she was 55 years of age. She successfully responded to the newly-founded Whipple Procedure for pancreatic cancer. We are celebrating thirty years since that emotional and life-altering day. My mom is truly a miracle and an inspiration at the active age of 85 years old. Today, she lives in an independent senior living complex and chooses to take the stairs to her third-floor apartment as opposed to the elevator. She does have type II diabetes due to the Whipple Procedure; however, her choice of colorful eating has enabled her to live the quality of life that she deserves. It truly does begin in the mind. My mom was not going to give in, and her mindfulness, positive attitude and never-ending smile continues to shine and inspire others.

I changed my eating patterns and began to exercise during my senior year of high school. I began to eat seeds, beans, fruits and vegetables. I taught an aerobic exercise class at a local gym and became more active in sports. I was addicted to a healthy lifestyle. I lost twenty pounds and maintained that lean weight through three pregnancies and menopause. I am still addicted, active and living life to the fullest at the young age of 54. I will always be addicted! This is my life choice! I want to live with a great quality of life; be active with my grandkids, continue to bike, golf and other activities. My digestive issues are no longer an issue and my Raynaud's symptoms have subsided.

Your genetic genes are a powerful "why." Will you succumb to them or will you create an awareness as to what steps you can take to control them the best that YOU can? Your endocrine, metabolic and chronological changes are also a powerful "why." Be mindful of these changes during your life so that you can be the best version of yourself. For instance, females in puberty start to see a curve develop in their waistline and when they go through menopause, their waist gets taken away. Men have the same battles as their testosterone levels decline and their belly expands, sometimes finding it difficult to see their feet. However, you can defy this process. I am holding on to my waist the best that I can with daily healthy choices, but I will embrace the life cycle. After all, it is just an outer shell that protects your inner health and beauty – the key is to live a daily healthy lifestyle and feel comfortable in your own skin. Learn to love yourself for what you are, change what you can and embrace those things that you cannot change. A word of advice to the younger generation; start a workout routine and apply healthy eating habits as soon as you can, since it is easier to sustain a healthy metabolism and a healthy lifestyle. However, it is never too late and any changes that you make regardless of your age can help you achieve your goals, defy gravity, increase your metabolism and overall mental and physical well-being.

Proper nutritional needs are crucial for the metabolic, environmental, physical, mental and chronological changes. Water and a healthy daily nutrition regimen are vital to your health as addressed in this book. Your nutritional choice to eat animal protein or become vegan is totally up to you. However, minimal red meat and more plants and colorful food can help reduce inflammation. Inflammation causes havoc on your living organs and overall health, and we are all at risk of it depending on the choices that we make. My food choices are plants and colorful food, wild-caught fish with no animal protein. This book addresses and embraces all nutritional choices but focuses on the benefits of plant, fruits and vegetables along with moving your body, mind health and being the best version of yourself.

I have been blessed to share and mentor the methods of Q2 for longevity and, most importantly, a better quality of life. After all, we only have one body and get one life - what choices will you make?

———❖———

Chapter One

What is Q2?

Q2 simply means Quality and Quantity. I first applied this method to teach my clients about food intake, but I came to realize that this formula can be applied to so many aspects of one's life. First, we need to explore the quality of life that you are living, and then visualize the quality of life that you want to live. The quantity equation will fall into place if you prepare your mind, have a clear vision of your goal(s) and then begin to apply those actions.

Over the years, I have worked with hundreds of clients, many that have achieved their goals and many that fell short of their goals. Ultimately, even the little changes that a person makes in their lives can make an impact for them to live a better quality of life. This is what I have instilled into my clients, and the perception of their ultimate goals may require redirection, a change in an area of their life that they may be unaware of.

I observed my clients' reaction, dedication, and motivation with each session. Some needed little instruction, some need more instruction. Documenting their food journals along with exercise became enlightening to some and gruesome to others. I designed a simple formula to help define the strengths and weaknesses of their behaviors and actions in order to avoid any roadblocks and obstacles of negative thinking.

First, we must rid ourselves of past expectations and start fresh. A clear vision and clear mind create a willing mind and a willing body. Through the course of the book, you will learn to ditch the diet, make time for yourself with exercise, food prep and mind time.

Second, reach your goals with positive steps toward permanent changes with realistic expectations. Again, a goal without action is just a dream. Learn to take action and responsibility for your life – after all, we only have one body, one life. So, get ready to take baby steps or make leaps and bounds to live the quality of life that you deserve.

Rid YOURself of Past Expectations by Creating an Awareness

Q2 is designed to relieve you of all past expectations of unhealthy, unrealistic diet and nutrition programs. There is no failure with this formula, because this is not some fad diet that you are on or off.

First, let's not use the word diet ever again. Diet has the word die in it. Diet consists of some sort of deprivation that could lead to many health issues. Diets are unrealistic. They usually consist of unnatural eating patterns that cannot be sustained.

I like to refer to what people call diet as Daily Healthy Nutrition. In other words, it is not something that you are on or off, it is the good choices that you make daily in order to fuel your body and mind. And they can be sustained – sometimes we just need a little guidance.

To start, remember diet simply means daily intake, nothing more. Life is all about choices. Life is about living. You have the power in your body and mind to make the right nutritional choices. Learning the basics of nutrition will assist you in these choices. And along the way, you will learn to eat to live – not live to eat.

We must purge our kitchen from all unhealthy foods, foods that make you sluggish, foods that cause inflammation, foods that cause havoc on your living organs, foods that will shorten your life. But, what are those foods? What are you putting into your body? That is why food documenting is important, at least for a little while, so that you are aware of your habits. Together we will find out what steps you need to take in order to live a daily healthy lifestyle.

The high-inflammation foods are whites; white flour, white sugar, hydrogenated oil and high fructose corn syrup. Also included are high-glycemic foods, man-made foods, foods with preservatives, foods that you don't even know what the ingredients are, even red meat. Keep in mind that animal meat, especially red meat, can cause inflammation within our bodies.

Second, we must learn to eat proper portion sizes evenly throughout the day. You wouldn't let your gas tank go empty or the fluid levels in your car to get low. That would cause your car to not work properly. Same with your body; feed your body properly so that it can perform efficiently and effectively.

Last, apply the Q2 method as a guidance tool to help you live a daily healthy nutritional lifestyle of Quality and Quantity.

Quality

"If it roams on the land freely, if it swims in the sea,
If it grows on the earth or if you can pick it off a tree."

- Donna Fatigato

These are the optimal food choices. No man-made foods. Eat plant-based and colorful, first and foremost, choose lean protein, healthy fats and complex carbohydrates. Omit or choose fewer fatty proteins, unhealthy fats and simplex carbohydrates. If you must choose animal protein and fish, then select grass-fed, non-GMO and wild caught.

Quantity

Watch your serving sizes. Read the food labels and educate yourself. Stick close to single serving sizes at meal or snack time, as this alone can sabotage your caloric intake.

For Example, One Serving equals the following:

- 1 cup vegetable or fruits
- 1 piece of fruit
- ½ cup grains, beans, pasta
- 2 eggs or 4 egg whites
- ½ cup Greek yogurt
- 5-6 oz. fish
- Nuts and seeds fit into your palm
- Meat and poultry is the size of your palm or a deck of cards

Q2 Hydrate and Metabolism

Hydrate

- Make water your choice of drink. Water flushes out your internal organs, aids in weight loss and balances metabolism. Drink half of your body weight in ounces.
- Limit coffee to one cup.

- Omit soft drinks. Regular soft drinks have a lot of sugar and diet has a lot of chemicals.

- Hot, unsweetened tea provides antioxidants, aids in fighting viral and bacterial infections and is a natural cleanser and detox.

- Lemon is also a natural cleanser and detox. It helps balance the acidity of the stomach and aids in food absorption. Add a slice of lemon to your water. You can also squeeze it on your salad and other food.

- Limes help break down the fat in the body. Again, add a slice of lime to your water or squeeze it on your food.

Metabolism

Your metabolism begins to slow as you grow older. If you create great habits when you are younger, you will have a healthier metabolism as you age. If you create bad choices in your life, your metabolism will slow down. However, it is never too late – it will just take a little more effort on your behalf. The only way to really know the level of your metabolism is to take a metabolism test. This eye-opening RMR (resting metabolic rate) test is non-invasive, takes a few minutes of time, and is available for a fee. You can evaluate your metabolism on your own by your sleeping habits, energy levels and distribution of weight, especially around your midsection. We all have our own metabolic rates, which is the caloric amount that our bodies use just to stay alive. Even at total rest, without moving, your body is using and ultimately burning calories just to breathe, circulate blood, digest food, think, blink and more. This process takes more calories than one may think, hundreds or even thousands. A healthy metabolism will burn calories even at rest, even if you do not work out. You burn additional calories by performing basic activities of daily living; brushing your teeth, typing on your computer, doing the dishes and even driving in your car.

Take this metabolism quiz to see what you can do to create not only a healthy metabolism, but a healthy lifestyle, achieve your goal(s) and live the quality of life that you deserve.

Answer Yes or No to the following questions:

1. Do you eat breakfast or a healthy shake within one hour after getting up in the morning?
2. Do you eat mostly fresh and unprocessed foods?
3. Do you eat 3 balanced meals and 2-3 healthy snacks throughout the day, every day?
4. Do all of your meals include color (mainly vegetable and some fruit) along with at least 3 ounces of protein and/or healthy grains?
5. Are most of your meals in the 250-350 caloric range?
6. Do you drink at least half of your body weight in ounces of water?
7. Is dinner the lightest meal of the day?
8. Do you eat slightly less on less active days and slightly more on more active days?
9. Do you perform strength training at least 2-3x a week and doing cardio 3-4x per week?
10. Are you walking at least 3,500 steps per day?
11. Are you getting 7-9 hours of sleep each night?
12. Do you allow yourself mindful time daily; meditation, yoga, education, read a book?

If you answered 'Yes' to any of the questions above, kudos! Keep up the great work! If you answered 'No' to any of the questions above, then begin changing those important metabolism factors to 'Yes'. However, if you have a lot to change, focus on one or two at a time; trying to change them all at once may be overwhelming and disappointing. Keep your eye on the prize, focus on your goal – rewrite or copy the questions and place it on your refrigerator or somewhere you will see them daily. This will help you to stay on track and ultimately reach your goal of daily healthy living.

Q2 Health and Exercise History

Your health and family history can impact your life, but even making little changes to your lifestyle can create positive steps in the right direction and possibly change your genetic path.

Answer yes or no to the following questions:

1. Are you under the care of a physician or other health professional?
2. Are you taking medications?
3. Is your waist larger than your hips?
4. Do you have high blood pressure?
5. Do you have high cholesterol?
6. Do you have a bone or joint problem that has been or could be made worse by exercise?
7. Have you ever experienced any chest pain associated with either exercise or stress?
8. Do you have a family history of any of the following conditions (heart disease, hypertension, abnormal EKG, heart attack, angina, gout, asthma, diabetes, high cholesterol or any other conditions?
9. Have you ever smoked?
10. Do you drink more than 16 oz. of caffeine per day?

11. Do you drink alcohol?

12. Do you live to eat?

13. Have you ever been on a nutritional plan/program?

14. Do you experience frequent weight fluctuations?

15. Do you have negative feelings toward or have you had any bad experiences with a physical activity program?

16. Do you start exercise programs but then find yourself unable to stick with them?

If you answered 'Yes' to any of the Health and Exercise History questions, you will have to work smarter to overcome those barriers. First, always consult your doctor before starting an exercise program. Second, listen to your body, and last, rid yourself of negative feelings and unrealistic expectations.

———❖———

Chapter Two

Client Stories

The Q2 formula that is explained throughout this book has helped many clients succeed and reach their goals. Each client has a unique story with shortcomings and road blocks that you may be able to relate to. Recognizing these habits and mindsets and then being willing to make the necessary changes are crucial for reaching a goal.

Lynnette was a stress eater who did not eat breakfast and ate minimally throughout the day. She worked long hours and her routine of work and eating became a vicious cycle. In our sessions, Lynette would not completely share her eating habits with me. She shared with me about not eating breakfast and how she had no time to eat at work. Educating Lynette on the importance of eating breakfast and fueling her body throughout the day was crucial, not only to achieve weight loss, but to achieve overall health. She recognized this and was able to make the change of incorporating breakfast. Eating throughout her busy work day was still a battle, however.

Then the secrets surfaced as she shared with me what happened when she came home from work. Now, the whole time I was training her, I could see that she was eating a healthy, well-balanced dinner;

fish/chicken, vegetable/salad and healthy grains. But before she ate this healthy meal, her routine and downfall were cake rolls – you know they come in a twin pack – chocolate-covered cake goodness. Lynette would come home from work stressed and famished and would grab the box of cake rolls out of the cabinet and feast. As I gently asked her how many she ate, she stated three. Lynette was so embarrassed and extremely emotional about her confession as she continued to reiterate three packages of cake rolls, which really meant six cake rolls. At this point she was sobbing, so I said to her, "You can continue to eat 6." She looked at me like I was crazy, as she knew this habit was sabotaging her goals and her health. When I told Lynette that she could still eat six, she stopped crying and became attentive because she truly loved her cake rolls. Or did she? It was absolutely a bad habit and part of her daily routine. It was crucial that I handle this delicate situation with sincerity and optimism. So, I continued, "Let me guess. You come home from work, famished and stressed. You go to the cabinet and take out the box of cake rolls and continuously eat them while you are still standing." Lynette said, "Yes."

I said, "Okay, this is what I would like you to try tomorrow. When you get home, take the box out of the cabinet, open one package and take out one cake. Put the rest away in the cabinet. Cut the cake roll into six pieces and put it on the table with a large glass of water. Sit down and put one piece in your mouth and really take your time to taste the flavor. You were shuffling them into your mouth before and not really tasting them and enjoying the flavor. Cleanse your palette with a sip of water. Put the second piece in your mouth and, again, take your time to savor the flavor. Take the time to let the signals of the flavors go to your brain. Continue on this same pattern, one sip of water and one savoring taste of the cake roll."

Lynette said, "Okay, thank you, I will try this."

At our next session, Lynette couldn't wait to share what had happened. She did what I had asked her to do, and by the time that she got to her fifth piece, she didn't want any more. Her routine became a habit induced with stress eating - not the love of cake rolls. Lynette began to think about the flavors of her healthy dinner that she had in store for her. She applied the same savor-the-flavor protocol with her healthy foods to enjoy completely. Needless to say, Lynette kicked her bad habit and is one my hugest success stories with the loss of 158 pounds over a two-year period.

Kick your bad habits
by recognizing and changing your routine.

Darrel was an athlete in high school and college. His 40s brought him a sedentary lifestyle with an extra forty pounds. He expected quick results with minimal changes, only to find out that this was unrealistic. Darrel answered yes to two of the twelve metabolism questions. His daily steps were in the danger zone of under 2,000 steps per day. Week after week, I asked him to work on changing one or two of them at a time. Trying to change all of them to yes at one time may be overwhelming and can result in giving up completely. After minimal changes and minimal results, reality hit, and Darrel was ready to make the necessary changes. I redirected his focus on the loss of forty pounds to the first ten pounds. Applying the necessary changes into his lifestyle became forefront, and we began to restructure his nutrition, exercise and mind set. The first ten pounds came off and we continued to work together, changing each metabolism question one at a time, challenging him with workouts and food prep and applying the Q2 methods.

The next ten pounds came off easier for Darrel as good habits started to form. He would slip a little, but then get right back on the focus of his goal. He noticed he had more energy and wanted to feel that way. He noticed he felt better when he was active versus inactive and his new goal was 10,000 steps per day. His confidence was high, just as in his athletic days. Darrel shed his third and fourth set of ten pounds by moving his body and eating colorful, balanced meals throughout the day. He joined a basketball league at the gym and his new lifestyle of healthy living was forefront.

***Reach YOUR goals by positive steps
toward permanent changes with realistic expectations.***

Liz was complex. She suffered from addiction triggered by negative relationships in her life. Her self-esteem bottomed out and she struggled to get through the day. She went to a rehabilitation facility a few times and had a whole professional team to help her get through her past and current struggles. After years of living a normal life, free from addiction, Liz was faced with medical issues and was forced to buckle down with healthier eating or severely suffer the consequences. Her blood sugars were out of control, she had a new-found heart murmur and was diagnosed with an autoimmune disease. At the time of her medical issues, she was taking my Pilates class. We talked extensively after a class, and she shared her medical issues along with her aspirations. One of her aspirations was to teach Pilates, and one of her major setbacks was her health.

Liz began to eat healthy and continued with the practice of Pilates. Her medical issues were now a part of her everyday life, but her awareness of change was forefront. She beat addiction - it took her three times, but she did it. She was strong, yet still lacked a confidence within her. Her medical issues were under control, and I encouraged her to follow her dream. Yet her lack of self-confidence was holding her back, with feelings of not being good enough.

That week, in class, everyone took a turn showing their favorite Pilates move and explained why they liked it. It was a very inspiring class for all and gave everyone a chance to participate without any pressure. After class, she asked me to mentor her, and so I did. Liz is now teaching Pilates in a different state. I miss seeing her in class, but I am so proud of her accomplishments and success.

Focus on the person that you are today so that you can be the person that you want to be tomorrow.

Debbie was a bubbly, full-of-life client who always had a smile on her face. She was a breath of fresh air even though she had succumbed to every fad and antic for weight loss. She was in denial of the simple, healthy methods of weight loss. She would rather try anything other than making the necessary changes from her metabolism quiz and her lifestyle. Debbie was willing to try quick fixes at the snap of a finger, and I began to make it my goal to rid her of the quick-fix mentality. She came to our workouts with so many ideas of quick weight loss; the day she showed up to session completely wrapped in plastic wrap, I knew we had to have a serious conversation.

Yes, Debbie came swishing into our session with every part of her body (except her head, thank goodness) wrapped in plastic wrap. It took everything I had not to laugh as she came in with a huge smile on her face, ready to be noticed. I asked, "Are we really going to do your session with you wrapped up like a mummy?"

She said, "Yes, why? You know it helps burn calories, reduces fat and shrinks cellulite?"

I simply said it would be more beneficial if you would put the effort into food prep, workouts and forming lifestyle changes, rather than wrapping your body.

We proceeded with the session as her movement became limited and she built up a fast sweat. With every swish, Debbie was determined in her mind to burn calories, reduce fat and shrink cellulite with the aid of the plastic wrap. Halfway through our session, she couldn't take it anymore; sweating and then itching. With the smile on her face, she started to peel off the plastic wrap. After all the fads, antics and diets that Debbie has tried, I'm happy to say that she is now living a healthy lifestyle. It took quite a while for her to realize that eating colorful food and moving her body as it was intended to do was the key to living healthy and reaching her goals.

Change your efforts to realistic solutions.

Joe was a muscle guy. Every day, he pounded weight after weight in the gym. He became so bulky that his decrease in flexibility and imbalance of muscle became evident. I asked Joe to keep an open mind as we added some Yoga/Pilates techniques into his routine. I explained that lifting weights will shorten his strong muscles and stretching will re-lengthen his muscles. Joe did keep an open mind until we were ten minutes in, and then he said, "This isn't for me, I can't do this, my body doesn't move like that." It was evident that his imbalance was so severe, with overworked quadriceps and chest muscles, and I knew that this was exactly what he needed.

Before he walked away, I gave him a challenge, a challenge that I knew that he could do. I challenged him to a 3-minute plank – and he did it! Feeling so good about the challenge, I then challenged Joe to an upward plank. This time I got on the floor and showed him and held it while he tried extensively to get in the position to support the upward plank. He struggled and was unsuccessful. I pointed out that by changing up his routine by adding stretching routines would open and release those tight muscles. After six months of working with Joe, he was able to touch his hands together behind his back, something that he has been unable to do for years. Joe turned his one-on-one training sessions into a regular weekly practice of Yoga. He has excelled in his weight lifting by incorporating extra back and hamstring workouts to help balance out his muscles, and yes, he can now hold the upward plank for several minutes.

Work on your weaknesses and fuel your strengths.

Linda would refer to herself as my most dedicated, unmotivated client. Her dedication and attendance at our training sessions were remarkable. However, she would come with a whole list of exercises that she didn't like – and this was a long list. This was Linda's 'Don't like - Won't do' list. Of course, I would find creative ways to get her to do the exercises on her list, knowing that people tend to not want to do certain exercises, usually are the exercises that they need to do to successfully reach their goal(s). I kept Linda in her comfort zone by implementing the exercises that she liked but incorporated some of the 'other' exercises for a challenge and to ultimately help her meet her goal. Now I'm not going to lie, we did keep some exercises on her 'Don't like – Won't do' list. There is a fine line between killer trainer mode and being compassionate about her feelings and what her body is telling her. Linda was right about being my most dedicated client, but how can someone so dedicated be unmotivated at the same time? In Linda's eyes, she may have seen herself as unmotivated, but the commitment to our sessions, and most importantly, the commitment to herself, made her highly motivated and successful in reaching her goals.

Keep an open mind!

Beth was apprehensive about practicing yoga due to her inflexibility. At least that is what I thought. After encouraging her further to incorporate some Yoga into our sessions, the truth surfaced. Beth shared with me that the basis of her apprehension was from a bad Yoga experience while on vacation. The details caused laughter between us as she shared her experience with me. Beth explained that during the entire Yoga class the instructor, with a very heavy accent, kept approaching her during class and saying, "Oh, you bad – Oh, you really, really bad." Beth, sharing the experience with me while mimicking the instructor, released laughter from the both of us. I assured her that I would focus on her form and flexibility, and there would not be any ridicule involved. Since then, we have incorporated Yoga into Beth's sessions. It has been a positive experience, and her form and flexibility have improved tremendously.

LET GO of past experiences!

Mary would share wellness news at each training session. However, the overload of taking every piece of tabloid information to heart can once again sabotage your goals and ultimately your health. Mary shared tabloid explosions like, "I can drink wine and eat chocolate because it is good for my heart" "You only need to do 20 minutes of cardio each day" "Crunches are not good for your back and neck" and so on. Now, don't get me wrong, some of this news is great and does have some truth to it. I asked Mary, wouldn't it make sense to focus on her well-being and goals, versus news for the general population? As we created Mary's plan, I reiterated, yes, you can have a glass of wine or a piece of chocolate occasionally, but in moderation. Two important factors here, occasionally and moderation, one ounce or small square of the darkest chocolate, and five ounces of wine, preferably red with the lowest sugar content. The key to these small treats is to continue to fuel your body with colorful healthy food and move your body as it was intended to.

Yes, a dose of twenty minutes of cardio each day is great advice, especially considering that a large mass of Americans do not even meet the minimal 20-minute daily recommendation. However, Mary's goal was weight loss, so this was not conducive for her. I encouraged her to double that time to minimally forty minutes and initiate clean, colorful eating. Yes, incorrect crunches can cause strain on the back and the neck, but exercises executed properly should not. Evaluation of alignment should be considered based on the individual's body type and fitness capability.

As I worked with Mary, I encouraged her to focus on her goals, her why and her lifestyle. After months of looking for answers, Mary's why became clear; her answers were within her, not the media, and she shed her first ten pounds. One year later, Mary was still sharing the breaking-news information, but the difference was she was in a different mindset, down 38 pounds and at her goal weight.

Get out of your own way.

⋘⋙

Becky asked me how my client Laura lost the weight and what she was doing to keep the pounds away. I told her that she exercises on a regular basis, incorporated weekly food prep and has established healthy eating habits. Becky had the exercising down, and even worked out with Laura occasionally, but she did not comprehend the importance of healthier eating. Laura, on the other hand, found balance in exercise and daily healthy nutrition – and found success. Becky appeared surprised and somewhat disappointed. She still wanted to hear something else. She longed for something else. She wanted to hear that she can still go to the local buffet and eat whatever she wanted, in the masses of whatever she wanted, because she earned it. After all, she was working out five days a week, so why not reward herself with whatever she craved?

I encouraged Becky to strive for a long-term solution, to continue with her dedicated workouts while applying daily healthy eating habits using the Q2 method – quality and quantity. The combination of healthy eating and moving your body is reasonable and attainable in the right mindset. I assured Becky that healthy nutrition is a huge factor for not only her overall health, but was the missing component for reaching her goals. The cycle of workout/some good nutrition, workout/bad nutrition put her metabolism in spin mode and left her body confused. Overall healthier eating will promote a greater quality of life, sleep, attitude, energy and self-awareness. This was something that Becky continued to struggle with – the nutrition part – eating healthy one day, then dipping back into bad eating habits. Her weight and health continued to be up and down.

Becky began to redirect her focus on a food and mood journal. She diligently documented her daily food intake along with her mood and energy levels. She noticed a pattern when she ate high-glycemic foods, foods that were high in saturated fat, and unhealthy browsing food, her energy levels were low, and her mood was either anxious, stressed or just downright tired. As we worked together, we focused on the positive days in her journal, the days she had the most energy and the days that she was happy, calm, and vibrant. This is how Becky wanted to feel and the gateway to reaching her health and personal goals. After one year of working with Becky, she beat that vicious cycle and has applied Q2 into her daily life. In turn, she shed 43 pounds, lowered her cholesterol and lost 6% in body fat.

You can't cheat with bad eating and expect positive results.

———◆———

Bob shared with me that he was concerned about eating fruits because of the sugar content. I always reiterate to eat your fruits and veggies. Yes, your concern is valid if you are not balancing your natural sugars, like in fruit, with lean protein. I shared some great green protein drink recipes with Bob, and he was still apprehensive. I then pointed out that it was the sugar content that he was getting within his diet that he should be concerned with, along with his occasional indulgences; ice cream, cake, cookies, alcohol.

In today's world, there is such a misunderstanding about fruit. In reality, fruits are packed with vitamins, minerals and antioxidants plus many phytonutrients (plant-derived micronutrients). Eliminate the unnatural sugars in your daily diet and start fueling your body with the natural sugars in fruit, along with vegetables, grains, legumes, and lean protein.

Fruits are nature's gift – fuel your body with nutritious fruits and balance out the natural sugar with lean protein.

———◆———

Q2

Chapter Three

Find Balance in Your Life – Q2 Balance Plan

"I don't have time" – that phrase, the reason, the why is the #1 excuse from my clients. You have to want it, you have to own it. Visualize the quality of life you would like to live. There is time, if it is important to you. Balancing your time is crucial and the most effective way for you to reach your goals.

Finding balance in YOUR life may not be as simple as you think. Being mindful and planning out your Q2 Balance Plan can help you manage balance in your life and ultimately reach your goals.

Draw or visualize three circles – then write Clarity in the first circle:

Clarity

First and foremost, we must provide Clarity. You may have a difficult time creating balance in your life if your brain is cluttered and unfocused or you do not have a clear vision of your goals. Have you ever heard of messy mind, messy life? You will have a hard time moving forward unless you clear your mind. I mean, come on – we live in a fast-paced world with so many tasks to juggle, pulled between family, work, friends. So, what can we do to find balance? Let's find out and start the Q2 Balance Plan with an exercise, an exercise that I practice weekly and incorporate into my teachings of mind/body practices like yoga and Pilates. Keep in mind that I kept this exercise short, but, it can be practiced and extended as needed.

Close your eyes for ten seconds. As you open your eyes, let your eyes stay soft. Allow your conscious mind to deflate from your day, your errands, tasks and responsibilities as you fall into a state of silence, peace and harmony. Shut out any outside noises, turn off your inside voices. Push away any negative thoughts or energy. As you replace the positive energy back into your mind, body and spirit and you store that light of energy within your heart – the light of peace, love, hope, courage and happiness. With an open spirit, notice the change of heart, physical well-being and mind set. Clarity goes way beyond being clear of your goals and vision. It begins in decluttering your mind, sorting it all out, to lead a path, in order to process your goal and vision.

Balance is the second circle – write or visualize Balance:

You will truly benefit if you write this down instead of visualizing, so grab a pen and paper. Balance is so important in not only your own physical, mental and spiritual well-being, but also when reaching your goals. Balance is the key component to provide stability. What are you balancing in your life right now? This circle will be interchangeable depending on what is going on in your life. Highlight this circle as we will come back to this circle later.

The last circle is Teamwork:

These are people that can help you in need, people that you work with, plan with and accomplish goals with. Sometimes you just can't execute everything on your own, so you build relationships with like-minded people or people that can assist you.

Next, draw or visualize two circles centered on top of the three circles.

The first circle – write Vision:

Having a clear vison of your goals should be forefront. Write your goals or design a vision board and display them where you can be reminded of them daily. What is your purpose, what is your why? Purpose and why go hand-in-hand with Vision. Knowing what you want and planning out how you are going to get there are crucial.

The next circle is Action – that's right, take Action! A goal without action is just a dream! Nothing will happen unless you put it into motion. What steps will you take to meet your goals? Make an hour appointment with yourself, just like you would when setting up your appointments to get your hair cut or going to the dentist. Use this hour appointment to move your body and prep colorful meals. If you start your hour with brain overload, uninspired or unmotivated, try the exercise that we did earlier, do some Yoga Down Dogs (See Page 70) and/or get your blood pumping by cardio movement. You will be amazed at how much more you are able to accomplish. After all, a moving body creates a more functional body and mind.

Draw one final circle on top – this one you will not achieve – unless everything else is in balance. Keep this circle blank for now:

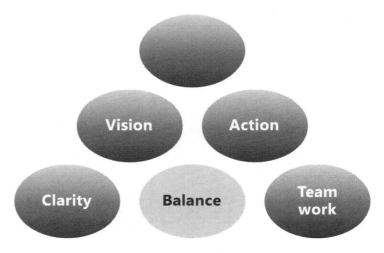

Now write or visualize the same six circles stacked up on top – we are going to write the groups, people, things, and activities that you are trying to balance in your life at this moment. What makes up your life? What does your day look like? What task/errands do you juggle daily? What areas do you need to work on to achieve your goals? For example, if your goal is to eat and live healthier, then you may balance your next set of circles, like so:

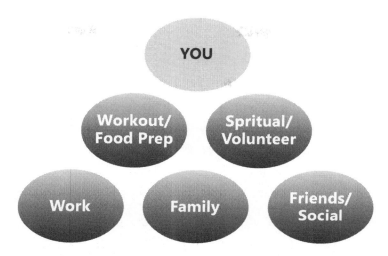

The first circle is work, as the average person will spend minimally forty hours at work each week. Work may also include taking care of your family, house, kids, cleaning, cooking, doing errands. Already you can see that as we stack our circles, our tasks and responsibilities in each circle may be more or less, depending on the attention needed in that area.

Family is the second circle, which is a stabilizer, a foundation – it is absolutely constant, but consistently fluctuates. Your family circle may contain taking care of a sick parent, balancing your children's schedules, family celebrations and gatherings, and the list can go on and on.

The third circle is Friends/Social, as it is important to keep your relationships healthy. Get out, laugh and enjoy life with friends and at social events. Social also may include social media where you can build relationships, nurture friendships, follow mentors, get support and even personal development. Social media is a way for people to get to know you and what your message is, but limit yourself on social media as it may be impairing your time in important areas needed in order to reach your goals. If social media ever radiates negativity in your life, then that is a sign to set limits and to work on yourself.

I look at the Workout/Food Prep as a filtering system that continually builds up your why, motivation and accountability. It can be taxing as you progress, but as you apply, you continually make room for more, until you have the consistency, while adding variety. Doing the same thing the same way and expecting changes is the definition of insanity. Change to what works for you and try something new as there are plenty of exercises and healthy food choices for you to explore.

Spiritual/Volunteer and helping others will create a positive direction in your life. Putting action into helping others can provide self-fulfillment while providing a positive impact on others' lives. In turn, you will create a message of hope, healing and transformation within them and within yourself.

The circle on the top is YOU! Highlight this circle! It is vital to make time for yourself. There is nothing in nature that blooms all year long, so don't expect to do so, either. We live in such busy lives, and it is important to slow down so we don't crash, misstep our goals, relationships or career. Take your off time as precious time to flourish your mind, body and relationships. Do what you love, move your body and fuel your mind.

So how are we going to tie this all in? Look at your two diagrams. This is where you are going to move YOU – the highlighted circle of the first diagram – Balance. So, the two diagrams will be on top of each other. Yes, YOU are Balance. The more you practice balance in all areas of your life, the more rounded you will become and your ability to achieve your goals will be greater. If you think about it, we are like computers – we sort, compute and place in folders and when new material comes up, we process and apply all over again. This is also like keeping a food journal, as you may not have a full awareness of what you eat until you start documenting. If you don't define what you need to juggle, then you will fall into the 'I don't have time' or 'I am too busy' category. I hear these two reasons from so many people, it's like a bad record skipping – that is never going to stop.

Let's recap. If your goal is to live a better quality of life, then have a clear vision of what YOU need to balance. Provide clarity in the mind, ask for assistance if needed, define your vision and purpose, then put it into motion – which leads us to the top blank circle. And yes, it is Success, but not just Success – always add repeat. Success and Repeat. There is no end. If you stop moving, you start dying. Success can come, but there is always another level, another need, another why, another fulfillment. Keep moving forward, never stop. Life is a journey.

You can use this same Q2 formula for what you would like to accomplish for the week to hold you accountable, or for other goals in your life. I tell the ladies at golf, "My golf game is like a box of chocolates, you never know what you are going to get." Well, that is pretty much how life is – you never know what is going to happen, what bump in the road you may encounter, but it is how you deal with it and learn how to sort it to fit into your life so you can still keep your eyes on the prize.

Whether you take baby steps or make leaps and bounds to live a healthy lifestyle will depend on YOU.

Attract balance in your life so that you can reach your goals with realistic expectations.

Chapter Four

Q2 Nutrition

Water Matters

Water is a vital element and nutrient. As stated prior, daily water intake should be half of your body weight in ounces. Why? Every part of your body is dependent on water; skin, brain, cells and organs. Optimal water intake can increase your energy, function and physical performance. Water helps break down the nutrients that you consume, carries them to your cells and then flushes the toxins out of your body, among other impurities. It's that simple, so grab your water and stay hydrated. But before you do, read further.

Quality and packaging of water has changed so much than in years past. The pollutants and uncertainty of safe drinking water is alarming. People want convenience, and the market for bottled water is on the rise but is also disturbing. Even the containers that we use can be doing more harm than good.

Filter your tap water for safety measures, and when buying bottled water, choose according to this order of purity – artesian, spring, then purified. Not only does water matter, but containers matter. Switch out your plastic water bottle for healthier solutions like reusable containers or bottles with stainless steel or ceramic interiors. If you must use plastic, then choose BPA-free, but be aware that use over time, heating and other factors may disrupt the quality and cause havoc on your health. Glass bottles are best but be aware that even the metal lids often contain an anti-corrosive epoxy lining that contains BPA.

BPA is a chemical and can be a hormone disruptor. BPA may be lurking in not only your plastic water bottles, but also in other household products, drinks and food. First, taste your water, and if has a plastic taste to it, don't drink it. Keep plastic bottles away from heat exposure, as heat tends to promote the leaching of chemicals, even in the safer types of plastics. Yikes!

Did you know that there is a number inside of a triangle on the bottom of your store- bought water bottles and containers? That is a recycling number but is also a guide to help you choose healthier water containers. Avoid numbers 3, 6 and 7, as they are an endocrine disruptor and a probable human carcinogen. Choose numbers 1, 2, 4 & 5 as they are safer plastics. Keep in mind that you should also not reuse plastic drink bottles that were intended for single use.

Rule of the thumb is to drink quality water when you feel thirsty and especially when your mood is impaired, you have trouble thinking, have a headache or other physical ailments or feel sluggish, as even a little dehydration can bring on these symptoms.

To Gluten or Not to Gluten

That's all you have been hearing about lately, gluten. Should you decide to gluten or not gluten? If you were diagnosed by a physician with celiac disease, a gluten intolerance or any other digestive issues and were told to not eat gluten, then the answer is easy, don't eat gluten. However, if you were told by a medical professional that you have a gluten intolerance or a gluten sensitivity and do not need to specifically stay away from gluten, then keep a food journal and be aware of what is really going on with you and your body's system. There are so many other foods that can be affecting you, like certain food allergies, or you may have suddenly become intolerant to lactose. Eliminate gluten temporarily then reintroduce to see if you have symptoms. If you are not eating gluten because you think it may be the key to weight loss, think again. Many gluten free foods on the market today consist of high calories – yes, it is gluten free, but you are basically wanting and yearning for those replacement foods and ending up with more calories. Fuel with plant and colorful food instead, and your cravings will subside.

Gluten is a composite of storage proteins stored together with starch in the endosperm of various grass-related grains like spelt, barley, rye, oats and wheat products. It is a gummy, binding ingredient that acts like glue. Think of it as holding the food together. Yes, it is ideal for baking and raising bread, but the question is, can your digestive system handle it? Even if it can, it all goes back to Q2 – Quality and Quantity. Allow yourself those foods that you love if you are eating right 90% of the time and you are more than likely getting the proper nutrition and ratio of macronutrients from your food.

Using plant-based gluten-free grains such as quinoa, buckwheat, millet, amaranth, brown rice, flax, teff and other whole grains will surely satisfy your cravings, fill you up and provide you with the proper nutrients that your body and cells need for optimal nutrition. Still confused as to what gluten does and if you should gluten or not? The rule of the thumb is to eat what your body was intended to eat. Don't overthink it or jump on the band wagon because everyone else is. Everyone's bodily systems react differently – stay on track to healthy eating by fueling with earth, tree, plant and sea and the whole gluten issue should not even surface. If it does, that is a red flag, and you should keep a food journal and seek a medical professional.

There is so much controversy on the positive benefits of gluten versus the negative effects of gluten on the body. Gluten may reduce the risk of colorectal cancer and may also have an effect on certain neurological disorders. These are only two of the benefits and effects, and there are many others. It truly comes down to awareness. Keep a food journal and learn the effects of food on your body and your mind. Everything should always be consumed in moderation. Apply these two things along with eating plant and colorful throughout the day and you will know what your body is telling you.

I have personally noticed in specifically my middle-aged clients, including myself, that the higher-grain bread, like 12-grain multi bread, is easier to break down and leaves an after effect of not feeling abundantly full or bloated versus 100% whole wheat bread. I stopped eating 100% whole wheat in my 40s because my body wouldn't and couldn't break it down. The 1/12th percentage in the 12-grain bread was fine, comfortable, doable and nourishing. I will eat gluten occasionally and it does not affect me, as I make sure that I eat a small portion along with colorful vegetables and lean protein throughout the day to balance it out. Keep in mind that I was not diagnosed by a medical professional and have taken it into my own hands to know my body and the effects of certain foods that I eat. Make it a priority to be aware and seek assistance if needed so that you can make your body a powerful and healthy machine.

Your Health begins in your Gut – Prebiotics and Probiotics

More than 2,000 years ago, Hippocrates stated: "All disease begins in your gut."

Today we are coming to realize how right he was and that gut health is critical to overall health, and an unhealthy gut can contribute to a wide range of diseases and directly inhibit you from reaching your goals. A growing body of research shows your gut microbiome (the scientific name for the trillions of microorganisms living in your digestive tract) may play a role in almost every aspect of health, including digestion, immunity, weight, heart health, and even memory. Nutritional research continues to pinpoint the importance of prebiotics and probiotics to sustain a healthy gut. By eating plant-based and colorful, without chemicals and man-made foods, you are more apt to naturally promote a healthy gut.

Prebiotics are natural, non-digestible carbohydrates that are linked to promoting the growth of good bacteria in your gut and can improve gastrointestinal health. Prebiotics feed the healthy bacteria (probiotics) in your gut to stimulate growth and promote balance. Choose foods that are readily available for absorption and digestion like raw chicory root, dandelion greens, endive, sunchokes, artichokes, asparagus, leeks, onions, garlic, soybeans, legumes, jicama, seaweed, blueberries, bananas, plantains, honey, oats and cereal grains (raw wheat bran, barley, rye).

Probiotics are microorganisms (live cultures) that help with digestion and offer protection from harmful bacteria, just as the existing good bacteria in your body already do. These active cultures help change or repopulate intestinal good bacteria to balance your complex microorganism system (gut flora) in order to boost your immune system and overall health. Often referred to as the 'friendly bacteria', probiotics are live microorganisms that we consume in fermented foods. Probiotics are believed to be beneficial to our health in many ways and can help alleviate irritable bowels, eczema and allergies. Drink fermented beverages like kefir or kombucha or choose bacterial fermentation foods such as yogurt, sauerkraut, lacto-fermented lentils, chickpeas or fermented soybeans (miso, tempeh, natto). Add fermented vegetables (kimchi, beets, green beans, carrots, pickles, traditional cured Greek olives) and raw apple cider vinegar to fuel your gut with friendly bacteria, the good bacteria that survive the aging process in some soft cheese like ricotta, Gouda, mozzarella and cottage cheese. It is important to look for live and active cultures on food labels.

I like to call prebiotics and probiotics P2, as they work as a powerful team. P2 works together synergistically; prebiotics as a good bacteria promoter, and probiotics as good 'live culture' bacteria. You can enjoy the combination of this powerful team by simply eating Greek yogurt with blueberries or whipping up a stir fry with prebiotic; asparagus, onions, edamame and probiotic; tempeh. (See Tempeh Stir Fry Recipe on page 224).

Prepare your kitchen with food that contain both prebiotic and probiotic, so they are readily available for absorption and digestion. Check out more healthy suggestions in the Q2 recipe section of this book.

Incorporate gut-health functional foods into your daily nutrition for a healthier YOU.

Macronutrients and Micronutrients

Our bodies depend on whole nutritional needs to survive, function and perform. The two vital nutrients are macronutrients (carbohydrates, protein and fat) and micronutrients (vitamins and minerals). The body requires the macronutrients in a larger amount (macro) to grow, develop, repair and feel good. Micronutrients are equally important and a necessity; they are required for optimal body function and production, but in a lesser quantity (micro).

All three **macronutrients** are important as each perform vital functions in the body. The trick is to understand how each macronutrient plays a different role in the body and how to incorporate the proper ratio of each in your daily nutrition. I like to follow the 40/45-25/30-25/30 rule; 40-45% healthy carbohydrates, 25-30% healthy protein and 25-30% healthy fats.

Carbohydrates are the main energy source of the human body. They are comprised of small chains of sugar which the digestive system breaks down into glucose to use as the body's primarily energy source. Carbohydrates are made up of three components: fiber, starch and sugar. I like to correlate the three components as a green light (fiber), yellow light (starch) and red light (sugar). The key is to choose the good carbs, known as complex carbohydrates, versus the bad carbs, known as simple carbohydrates. Complex carbohydrates are comprised of fiber and starch and are nutritionally more favorable than simple sugars, because they are higher in fiber and therefore digest slower. Fiber is especially important because it promotes bowel regularity, digestive health and helps to control cholesterol. Some of the best food sources of dietary fiber include vegetables, fruits, whole grains, nuts and beans. The starchy carbs are considered more starchy than fibrous, like potatoes, whole wheat bread, peas, corn and rice.

Simple carbs are sugars comprised of refined sources and sugar additives and can have a negative impact on one's health. Intake of simple sugars can spike your sugar levels and contribute to food cravings, weight gain, mood changes, restlessness, headaches and other medical issues like diabetes and heart disease. Avoid simple carbohydrate foods like soda, packaged cookies, baked treats and even breakfast cereals that are loaded with simple sugars. Sugar additives to be aware of are some familiar ones, like fruit juice concentrate, brown sugar, corn syrup and especially high-fructose corn syrup, but also the many sugar additives that are on the market today. There are thousands of 'safer' food additives and any one of them could end up on your plate. Read the food labels or better yet, eat fresh – Earth, tree and plant to create a powerful positive impact on your health.

Carbohydrates Food Group	Quality Food Choice Examples	Quantity One Serving = One Item
Grains (3-5 servings daily)	Unprocessed: Oats, brown rice, barley, millet, bulgur wheat, multi-grain, quinoa	1 slice bread ½ cup hot cereal / oats ¼ cup granola ½ cup rice or pasta
Vegetables (4-6 servings daily)	All fresh: Kale, spinach, collards, broccoli, cabbage, pumpkin, carrots, zucchini, sweet potatoes, potatoes, parsnips, rutabagas, turnips, beets, tomatoes, eggplant, okra, squash, cauliflower	1 cup raw, leafy vegetable salad ½ cup chopped raw vegetables ½ cup cooked vegetables
Fruits (3-5 servings daily)	All fresh: Lemons, limes, raspberries, blueberries, strawberries, apples, pears, peaches, apricots, plums, oranges, grapefruit, kiwi, mango, papaya, persimmons, pineapple, banana Dried fruit: Prunes, dates, figs, raisins, cranberries	1 medium, whole fruit 1 cup chopped fruit 1 cup berries ¾ cup natural fruit juice ¼ cup dried fruit
Beans	Any type of bean; Adzuki, black, black-eyed, fava, garbanzo beans, great northern, kidney, lentil, lima, mung, navy, pinto, soybean, split pea, white, green beans, snow peas	½ cup cooked beans/peas

Each carbohydrate has a glycemic index (GI) rating. If you are eating fresh, non-man-made food then most likely you are eating low- to medium-glycemic. If you are not, however, then you may be doing more damage to your body than you thought. Here is an easy way to understand the glycemic index and the effects that it has on your body, organs and system.

The rating is based on how quickly the carbohydrates are used in your body. The faster a carbohydrate is used the more of a spike it will produce on your blood sugar (insulin levels). This is high-glycemic. However, a low-glycemic food will not produce significant insulin spikes; it is kinder to your system, fuels your metabolism and regulates your hunger.

Knowledge is power. Healthy eating comes from knowledge, the effects of the food and then planning your meals accordingly. For instance, basmati rice has a GI rating of 52, and anything under 55 is considered low-glycemic. Brown rice and arborio rice (risotto) have a medium-glycemic index rating and white rice has a high-GI rating of 79. Black rice is also low-glycemic, but provides extra protein, fiber and even antioxidants, compared to these other types of rice. Continued intake of high-glycemic food can cause insulin resistance which, in turn, can sabotage your health and goals. Still confused? Read on.

Insulin resistance is a process where our bodies do not let insulin work. Insulin has many jobs in our body. Insulin allows blood sugar to enter our cells. With a poor diet, high-glycemic food, lack of exercise, and genetic factors, our bodies become resistant to the actions of insulin, so our bodies try to compensate and secrete more and more insulin to get blood sugar into the cells. But insulin also acts as a storage hormone, and when we have high levels, our fat cells are told to store fat and not burn fat, so we gain weight. This is how insulin resistance contributes to weight gain. It is not the carbohydrates, per se, but it is the effects of eating high glycemic vs. low glycemic, improper macronutrient ratio and the overall lifestyle that we lead.

Protein is essential for repairing and regenerating body tissues and cells, manufacturing hormones and promoting a healthy functioning immune system. Amino acids are the building blocks of protein, as their key role is the transport and proper storage of nutrients. There are twenty types of amino acids, however, nine of which are essential that can only be found in protein-based foods. I personally do not eat animal protein, as that is my personal choice. If you eat animal protein, choose the leanest cuts of meat, pork and poultry and cut back on your red meat intake. Follow the rule of Q2, earth, tree, land and sea. Incorporate the following protein-rich plant-based foods in your daily nutrition; quinoa, beans, legumes, seeds (chia, flax, hemp), nuts (almonds, walnuts), avocado, beets, and raw greens like spinach and kale.

Protein Food Group	Quality Food Choice Examples	Quantity One Serving = One Item
Beans, Nuts, Seeds (3-4 servings daily)	Navy beans, edamame, lentils, northern beans, kidney beans, mung beans, split peas, garbanzo beans (chickpeas), black-eyed, adzuki, fava, lima, pinto, white beans, Almonds, almond butter, walnuts, pistachios, cashews, cashew butter, hazelnuts, pine nuts -Hemp seeds, flax seeds, pumpkin seeds, sunflower seeds, sunflower butter	½ cup cooked beans/peas 1/8-1/4 cup nuts ¼ cup seeds
Grains	Wheat germ, quinoa, soba noodles, black rice	½ cup quinoa/black rice
Milk	Greek yogurt, cottage cheese, ricotta cheese, Swiss cheese, mozzarella, goat cheese	½ cup yogurt ¼ cup cottage/ricotta cheese 1 oz. cheese
Other	Tempeh, tofu, eggs, beets, plant protein powder	1 egg or 2 egg whites
Seafood	Yellow fin tuna, halibut, octopus, sockeye salmon, anchovies, sardines, water packed light tuna preferably in a glass jar	5-6 ounces
Meat, Pork, Poultry	Grass-fed beef, corned beef, roast beef, Canadian bacon, chorizo, pork chops, boneless/skinless chicken, turkey breast	3-4 ounces

Fats provide essential fatty acids to help protect the body's organs, improve brain development, encourage overall cell functioning and aid in absorbing vitamins found in foods. Dietary fats dissolve and transport fat-soluble nutrients, such as some vitamins and disease-fighting phytochemicals like carotenoids, alpha- and beta-carotene and lycopene. Don't be afraid of eating fats – choose healthy fats like almonds, walnuts, avocados, olives and seeds (pumpkin, sunflower, chia). And if you Sea, remember that fats are a combination of fatty acids, so even healthy fish contain some saturated fatty acids. The combination of fatty acids outweighs the sole saturated fat of its contents. Enjoy foods with monounsaturated and polyunsaturated fats (green light) while limiting the unhealthy saturated (yellow light) and excluding the trans fats (red light).

Review the following information on various fats so that you can have a clear vision of what choices and changes should be made to your daily nutrition:

Unsaturated Fats (green light). There are two classes of unsaturated fatty acids: monounsaturated fats and polyunsaturated fats. These are the right or healthy unsaturated fatty acids that your body can truly benefit from by improving blood cholesterol levels and insulin sensitivity while protecting your arteries and heart. Monounsaturated fat sources include avocados, nuts, seeds and olives and referred to as MUFAs. PUFAs are commonly known as polyunsaturated fats that consist both omega-3 fatty acids and omega-6 fatty acids, but each has a different role in the body. ALA (a-Linolenic acid) is an omega-3 fatty acid that your body is unable to create, so it is essential that you get it in your diet with such foods as walnuts, tofu, soybeans and ground flaxseed. Your body also makes two other critically important omega-3 fatty acids, EPA and DHA. Not only is ALA important for heart disease prevention, but EPA and DHA are also important for heart health. EPA and DHA can be found in fish, like mackerel, lake trout, salmon, sardines and tuna. They also promote visual acuity, slow the rate of cognitive decline in the elderly, promote brain development in the fetus and youth and contain anti-inflammatory agents that may decrease the symptoms of inflammatory diseases. LA (linoleic acid) is an omega-6 fatty acid and needs to be acquired through food. Sources of omega-6 fatty acids are sunflower seeds, pecans, pine nuts, sunflower and sesame oil.

Saturated Fats (yellow light). Your body is an incredible piece of equipment and can make all the saturated fatty acids that it nutritionally needs. It's when you have an overabundance of unhealthy saturated fats, like full-fat cheese, pizza and desserts, that you increase the risk of high cholesterol, heart disease and other medical conditions. Other saturated fats to stay away from are ones where they harden the oil in a process called hydrogenation, usually to increase the shelf life of processed foods, yet another reason to eat Earth, tree, land, sea. Choose low-fat cheese, nuts, and fish, and switch out desserts for almond butter and fruit.

Trans Fats (red light). Your body reacts to what you eat, and trans fats trigger insulin resistance, raise the bad cholesterol (LDL) but also lower the good cholesterol (HDL) which can lead you into a whole host of medical issues. The trans fats are the health-damaging fats as they serve as a precursor of hydrogenation, hardening of the oil, to increase shelf life. Partial hydrogenation converts some, but not all, unsaturated fatty acids to saturated ones. It's the ones that remain unsaturated but are changed in chemical structure that are artery-scarring fats, such as cakes, pies, cookies, biscuits, margarine, doughnuts, fried fast foods and many man-made foods.

Healthy Fats Food Group	Quality Food Choice Examples	Quantity One Serving = One Item
Beans, Nuts and Seeds	Edamame (soybeans), tahini (sesame seed butter), walnuts, almonds, pecans, macadamia, pumpkin seeds, flax seeds, chia seeds, olive oil, coconut oil, coconut, almond butter, cashew/sunflower butter	½ cup cooked beans 1/8-1/4 cup nuts ¼ cup seeds 2 T. almond/cashew butter
Other	-Tempeh, tofu, egg yolks, avocado -Greek yogurt, milk -Cheese; cottage, ricotta, goat, Swiss, mozzarella, feta -Honey, agave nectar -Highest % dark chocolate	½ cup tempeh ½ avocado ½ cup Greek yogurt ¼ cup ricotta/cottage cheese 1 oz. cheese 1 T. honey/agave nectar 1 oz. dark chocolate
Land & Sea and Meat Substitutes	Beef, pork shoulder, ham, duck, dark meat chicken, dark meat turkey, nitrate-free deli-slices, wild salmon, tuna	3-4 oz. animal protein 5-6 oz. seafood
Vegetable Fats and Oils	-Olive oil, avocado oil, sour cream, cream cheese, butter	1 T. oil 1 T. butter

The bottom line is fuel your body with colorful fresh food and plant-based foods known as phytonutrients. **Phytonutrients** are found in fruits and vegetables and other plant-based foods such as whole grains, nuts, beans and tea. These powerful phytonutrients are believed to be beneficial to human health and can help prevent various diseases and medical conditions. Phytonutrients are the common denominator in the above information for healthier eating and overall health. There are thousands of phytonutrients found in plant foods. See the chart below for the sources and benefits of six important phytonutrients.

Phytonutrient	Function	Source	Food Sources
Carotenoids; Alpha-carotene Beta-carotene Beta-cryptoxanthin	-Act as an antioxidant as they tackle harmful free radicals that damage tissues throughout the body -Linked to a lower risk of prostate cancer. -Protect from cataracts, macular degeneration	Vitamin A Lycopene Lutein/ Zeaxanthin	-Yellow and orange foods like carrots and pumpkins -Red or pink foods like watermelon, tomatoes & grapefruit -Green foods like spinach, kale and collards
Ellagic acid	Ellagic acid may help protect against cancer and slow the growth of cancer cells	Polyphenols	-Strawberries, raspberries and pomegranates
Flavonoids Catechins Hesperidin Flavonols	-May help prevent some types of cancer -An antioxidant that reduces inflammation -May help reduce risk of asthma, some cancers and coronary heart disease	Quercetin	-Green tea -Citrus fruits -Apples, berries, kale and onions
Glucosinolates	The chemicals released during the cooking process or when digested can slow the growth of cancer	Cruciferous Veggies	-Brussels sprouts, cabbage, kale and broccoli
Phytoestrogens	Can exert estrogen-like effects or block the effects of your natural supply of estrogen for lower risk of endometrial cancer and bone loss in women	Isoflavones Lignans	Soy Foods like tofu, soybeans and tempeh Sesame seeds and flaxseeds
Resveratrol	Acts an antioxidant & anti-inflammatory. May reduce the risk of heart disease and certain cancers.	Natural phenol	Purple grape juice, grapes, blueberries and red wine

Eat a rainbow every day for optimal health and overall well-being.

Micronutrients are essential non-caloric, organic nutrients that are a small part of daily nutrition. The role of the micronutrients is to help make possible the processes by which other nutrients are digested, absorbed and metabolized or built into body structure. Micronutrients can be broken down into two categories: fat soluble and water-soluble. There are four fat-soluble vitamins, vitamin A, D, E and K. These vitamins are absorbed like fats, first in the lymph, then the blood stream. They are not readily excreted and tend to build up in the tissue. They are found in fats and oils of food and are stored in the liver and fatty tissues until they are needed. Deficiencies can occur when people eat diets that are low in fat and unhealthy diets. Special groups can also be at a higher risk:

Fat-Soluble Vitamins	Function	Quality Food Sources	Groups at higher risk due to Deficiencies
Vitamin A *Supplies three forms of retinoids:* -Retinol stored in the liver. The liver makes retinol available to blood and then cells. -Cells then convert retinol to retinal and retinoic acid as needed for reproduction.	-Immune defenses -Normal development of cells -Growth of bones and of the body -Maintenance of body linings and skin -Reproduction -Gene expression -Vision	-Sweet Potato -Spinach/Broccoli -Carrots/Pumpkin -Cantaloupe -Sweet Red Peppers -Mangos/Apricots -Black-eyed peas -Ricotta Cheese -Tomato juice -Atlantic Herring	-Pregnant women -Crohn's disease -Celiac disease -Cystic Fibrosis -Cancer -Age-related macular degeneration

Vitamin D *This vitamin can be self-synthesized with the help of sunlight.* -Whether made with help with sunlight or obtained from food, vitamin D undergoes chemical transformations in the liver and kidneys.	-Acts as a hormone to regulate blood calcium/phosphorus levels to maintain bone integrity -To replenish blood calcium, vitamin D acts at three body locations to raise blood calcium levels; skeleton, kidneys and digestive tract	-Sunlight -Cod liver oil -Swordfish/ Salmon -Tuna/Sardines -Shrimp/Oysters -Mushrooms/Tofu -Oatmeal -Greek Yogurt -Egg yolks -Milk/Swiss cheese -Goat/Ricotta cheese	-Breastfed infants -Older adults -Obese people -Dark complexion -Limited sun exposure -Those with fat malabsorption -Those that have undergone gastric bypass surgery
Vitamin E *A protector of free radical and oxidative damage.* -Compounds like tocopherols and tocotrienols.	-An Antioxidant -Can neutralize free radicals -Gene expression -Prevent damage to cells -Eye & neurological functions -Protects lipids	-Wheat germ -Sunflower seeds/ oil -Almonds/ Hazelnuts -Almond butter -Olive & Soybean oil -Spinach/Broccoli -Kiwifruit -Mango -Tomato	-Unhealthy -Occurs in premature babies born before the transfer of the vitamin from the mother to the infant, which takes place in the last weeks of pregnancy
Vitamin K *Main function is to help synthesize proteins that help blood clot.* -Vitamin K can be made by healthy intestinal bacteria.	-Necessary for the synthesis of key bone proteins -A dose of vitamin K is suggested for newborns at birth to help blood to clot and lessen the risk of vitamin K deficiency bleeding	-Turnip greens -Broccoli/ Asparagus -Cabbage/Spinach -Green Tea -Watercress/Peas -Green Beans -Milk/Eggs -Tomato/Potato -Banana/Orange -Bread/Butter	-Celiac disease -Ulcerative colitis -Biliary obstruction -Short bowel syndrome -Intestinal resection -Cystic fibrosis

Water-soluble vitamins are not stored in the body, so it is important to provide an adequate supply through a balanced daily nutrition plan. There are nine water-soluble vitamins, the eight B-complex vitamins and vitamin C. They have many functions, roles, food sources and at risk of deficiency:

Water-Soluble Vitamins	Function	Quality Food Sources	Groups at higher risk due to Deficiencies
Vitamin C *A protector of free radicals generated during the assault on invaders and assists enzymes involved in the formation of collagen.* -Vitamin C is ascorbic acid and necessary for the production and repair of tissues throughout the body.	-An antioxidant -Protects the immune system cells from free radicals -Assists enzymes involved in the formation of collagen -Promotes healthy collagen, the chief protein of most connective tissues including tendons, ligaments, blood vessels, scar tissue and the matrix upon which bone and teeth are built -Heals wounds and maintains bones	-All fruits & veggies -Red Pepper (raw) -Guava, Kiwi -Broccoli (raw) -Brussel Sprouts -Papaya/Strawberry -Orange/Lemon -Cantaloupe -Cauliflower -Spinach/Cabbage -Grapefruit -Raspberries -Tangerine	-Scurvy -High blood pressure -Stroke -Atherosclerosis -Gallbladder disease -Some cancers Deficiency symptoms may include; -Loss of appetite -Growth cessation -Bleeding gums -Swollen ankles/wrists -Anemia -Red spots on skin -Weakness -Loss of teeth
Vitamin B1 - Thiamin	-Strengthens the immune system -Helps promote normal appetite	-Nuts, healthy meats, fish, oatmeal, brown rice, vegetables, potatoes, liver, eggs	
Vitamin B2 – Riboflavin *Helps convert B6 and folate into active forms in the body*	-An antioxidant -Necessary for healthy vision	-Brewer's yeast, whole grains, organ meats, dairy products, bananas, green beans, asparagus	-Cataracts -Macular degeneration

Vitamin B3 – Niacin	-Helps produce hormones -Improves circulation -Reduces levels of bad cholesterol and increases the good	-Eggs, poultry, nuts, enriched bread, mushrooms	
Vitamin B5 – Pantothenic Acid *Helps the body use riboflavin. Needed for the synthesis of cholesterol.*	-Vital for the production of red blood cells and steroid hormones -Needed for synthesis of cholesterol	-Avocados, potatoes, vegetables in the cabbage family, broccoli	In a B Vitamin deficiency, every cell is affected. Symptoms may include:
Vitamin B6 – Pyridoxine *Helps produce the chemicals that nerves use to communicate with one another.*	-Critical for the nervous system, brain development and function and blood cell production. -Reduces the levels of homocysteine in the blood to protect from cardio disease	-Avocados, bananas, meats, vegetables, nuts	-Nausea -Irritability -Depression -Forgetfulness -Severe exhaustion -Loss of appetite and weight
Vitamin B7 – Biotin *Also known as vitamin H*	-It assists in metabolic reactions -Helps maintain levels of blood sugar	-Legumes, nuts, milk, some vegetables	-Impairment of immune response -Abnormal heart action -Skin problems
Vitamin B9 – Folate / Folic Acid *Assists in DNA / RNA production and controls levels of homocysteine*	-Critical for the brain and mental health -Works with B12 to regulate the forming of red blood cells and help iron function	-Beets, legumes, peanuts, green leafy vegetables, pasta, whole grain bread	-Swollen red tongue -Teary, red eyes -Pain in muscles
Vitamin B12 – Cobalamin	-Vital for metabolism -Plays a role in the formation of red blood cells and helps maintain the central nervous system	-Animal proteins including meats, fish, eggs and milk	

Macro minerals are needed in the human body in a larger dose and are essential for a healthy body and a healthy life. Some of the big hitters include calcium, potassium, magnesium, phosphorus, sodium and sulfur:

Macro Minerals	Function	Quality Food Sources	Groups at higher risk due to Deficiencies
Calcium	-Essential for healthy bones and teeth -Helps muscles relax and contract -Essential to nerve functioning, blood clotting, blood pressure, regulation, immune system health	-Salmon, sardines, tofu, soy milk, milk products, legumes, mustard greens, broccoli, spinach, figs	-Osteoporosis -Osteopenia
Magnesium	-Needed for making protein, muscle contraction, nerve transmission, immune system health	-Legumes, seeds, nuts, leafy green vegetables, seafood, artichokes	-Crohn's disease -Celiac disease -Diabetes
Potassium	-Needed for proper fluid balance, nerve transmission and muscle contraction	Fruits, vegetables, whole grains, milk, legumes, meat	-Those on water pills or diuretics
Phosphorus *Found in every cell; part of the system that maintains acid-base balance*	-Essential for healthy bones and teeth	-Eggs, milk, fish, poultry, meat	-Osteoporosis -Osteopenia
Sodium	-Needed for proper fluid balance, nerve transmission and muscle contraction	-Liquid amino acids, sea salt plus small amounts in milk, meat, breads, vegetables	-Hyponatremia (low sodium)
Sulfur *Occurs in foods as part of protein*	-Found in protein molecules	-Eggs, milk, legumes, nuts, fish, poultry, meat	

Micro minerals or trace minerals are essentials in a much lower dose, however, and they all play a vital role for overall health. Some of the mighty little hitters include zinc, iodine, selenium, copper, manganese, chromium, molybdenum, iron:

Micro Minerals	Function	Quality Food Sources	Groups at higher risk due to Deficiencies
Zinc *A part of many enzymes needed for making protein and genetic material*	-Taste perception -Wound healing -Production of sperm -Normal growth -Immune system health -Normal fetal development	-Pumpkin seeds, chickpeas, lentils, legumes, nuts, fish, poultry, whole grains, vegetables, meat	-Pregnant women -Those that take diuretics or misuse alcohol -Diabetes -Long term liver disease -Long term kidney disease
Iodine *Found in thyroid hormone*	-Regulates growth, development and metabolism	-Seafood, iodized salt and foods grown in iodine-rich soil, bread, dairy products	-Hypothyroidism
Selenium	-An antioxidant	-Seafood, grains, meat	-Crohn's disease
Copper *Part of many enzymes needed for iron*	-Regulate metabolism	-Legumes, seeds, nuts, whole grains, organ meats, drinking water	-Anemia -Osteoarthritis -Osteoporosis
Manganese *Part of many enzymes*	-Regulate metabolism	-Plant foods	-Osteoporosis -Anemia -PMS
Chromium *Works closely with insulin*	-Regulates glucose levels (blood sugar)	-Whole grains, nuts, cheese, brewer's yeast, liver	-Diabetes -Glaucoma

Molybdenum	-Regulate metabolism	-Legumes, bread and grains, leafy greens, green vegetables, milk, liver	-Those whose diets rely mainly on processed or refined foods
Fluoride	-Formation of bones and teeth -Helps prevent tooth decay	-Fish, tea and drinking water that has fluoride	-Dental caries -Osteoporosis
Iron *Part of a molecule (hemoglobin) found in red blood cells*	-Carries oxygen in the body -Energy metabolism	-Chickpeas, lentils, fish, poultry, meat, egg yolks, legumes, dried fruits, dark leafy greens, iron-enriched bread/ cereal	-Anemia

Other trace nutrients known to be essential in tiny amounts include silicon, nickel, vanadium, and cobalt.

Optimal Cellular Nutrition -Antioxidants and Minerals

I believe in getting your antioxidants and minerals from food first — fueling your body with colorful phytonutrients, protein and healthy fats. If you choose the correct healthy food sources, will you be covered with optimal cellular nutrition? Even if you eat 100% healthy, which is a great challenge to achieve in today's world, our foods and crops are depleted of nutrients compared to those in years past. The only other way to make sure that you are fueling your cells with optimal nutrition is with supplementation. However, all supplements are not rated the same.

Just like your food sources, know where your supplements come from before making your decision. If you are not currently taking a multi-vitamin, antioxidants and minerals, which cover your complete nutritional needs from A to Z, then think again. The breakdown of vitamins and minerals in the Macronutrients and Micronutrients section of this book gives you plenty of reasons why they are important for overall health and ultimately a greater quality of life. Even the American Medical Journal states, "It is prudent that all Americans take a Multi-Vitamin." Whether you are new to the use of nutritional supplements or currently on a supplement regimen, please know the answers to the following four questions.

1. **What is the binding agent of the product?**

    Yes, supplements have binders and some even have fillers. Some mass-produced vitamins are bound with petroleum and crude oil. Yikes! That is a red flag in my book. I choose a supplement that is bound with olive oil from the olive plant, which has many heart and health benefits.

2. **Where is it manufactured?**

    Some mass-produced companies not only manufacture their own products, but also for other supplement companies. Ask the question of what else is manufactured at the plant, as the environment can interfere with the substance of the product. I choose a company that is a FDA-registered facility that solely manufactures their own products in an environment with one goal – optimal cellular nutrition.

3. **How is the product rated according to quality, purity and potency?**

    Is the product pharmaceutical grade? How many times is the product tested before bottling and is the label on the bottle the actual ingredients in the product? I choose a company that tests their product 5-7 times before bottling and guarantees that what is on the label is 100% in the product.

4. **What is the background of the company?**

Did the company originate as a business venture or with a medical/scientific background that has a common goal to help others achieve optimal nutrition? Find out why and how the company began and what their goals are. I choose a company whose founder is an immunologist and microbiologist, a recipient of the Albert Einstein Award for Life Sciences that facilitates a large scientific and athletic advisory board. Their goal is to provide safe optimal nutrition and ultimately a better quality of life.

If you do not know the answers to the above questions, please find out. Knowledge is power. We cannot just assume in today's world that because they are on the market, they are okay to ingest. To the consumer, specials like buy one, get one free are appealing, but is it worth the risk of deficiency of quality, purity and potency of the product?

After all, we only get one body, one life – make it matter and choose wisely.

Q2 Plan when Dining Out

First off, try to eat out minimally and avoid fast food all together. I get it – eating out is social and an area in your life that brings joy as you bond with friends and family. However, being aware and then choosing the right type of food can bring mutual enjoyment, while keeping you on track to a healthy life.

Enjoy a salad while others eat appetizers! And while you are at it, ask for lemon to squeeze on your salad versus the calorie-dense salad dressing – otherwise, choose a vinegar or balsamic-based dressing. Going to cheat? Be strong – stay away from the fried and unhealthy choices. Order your favorite dressing on the side and dip your fork in the dressing before piercing your salad to minimize the quantity while enjoying the fresh flavors.

Avoid MSG (Monosodium Glutamate), fried or battered, bacon, cream sauces, sour cream, cream cheese, butter, mayonnaise, bread crumbs and anything stuffed with cheese. Choose entrees without cheese, but if you must, ask for 'less cheese'.

Substitute vegetables or sweet potato instead of whipped white, double-baked or french fries. Make sure they are steamed vegetables versus sautéed, so that extra unwanted calories and fat do not end up on your plate.

Be inquisitive. Ask where they get their meat or fish. You are the consumer and have the right to know what you are putting into your body. Choose grass-fed meat and poultry and wild caught fish versus GMO (genetically modified) injected meat and poultry and farm-raised fish. Ask how it is prepared and be ready to order without butter, sauce or cheese and to your healthy liking.

Follow these simple five steps:

1. **Choose plant based and colorful** – add a wise protein source if you wish.

   For example: Halibut with lemon wedges, steamed vegetables and dry sweet potato. That's right, nix the butter, brown sugar and marshmallows on the sweet potato – sweet potatoes are naturally sweet. Enjoy all of the natural and colorful flavors!

2. **Drink water and avoid alcohol**.

So, you may want to order alcohol to be more social. Order your water with one lemon and one lime and enjoy your healthy beverage, no one will know. You can even ask for it in a fancy glass. If you must cheat, then limit yourself to one cocktail - but choose wisely and always drink water with your adult beverage.

3. **Avoid the bread basket and hot rolls.**

No bread, no butter – plus more room to fuel your body with healthy food. Eating bread may also encourage you to eat more as it is a starch 'crave' carbohydrate.

4. **Only eat half of your meal and bring the other half home**.

Wait! What? Why? Choose healthy plus bring the other half home? Yes, simply because most restaurants serve a generous amount of food – sometimes double or even more double than a serving size. Unless you are at a small-plate restaurant, which by the way can be deceiving – small does not mean healthy, small does not mean less calories. Get into your mindset and split your meal in half right away. Think of it as two meals, one to enjoy now and one to enjoy later. Really take the time to savor the flavors of your food while sipping on your water. This is social, right? Then go slow, take your time, make it last and enjoy!

I like to use the following analogy . . .

Think of your stomach like a balloon – the more air you put in, the bigger the balloon grows. Same as your stomach – your stomach only needs a serving size, not double or more. The more you eat in one sitting, the more your body will want and crave. You are better off eating half of your meal and if you still desire the other half, then eat it an hour later rather than eating it all at once.

5. Forget about the dessert!

You chose healthy, so why sabotage your meal now! If you follow the first four steps, you most likely will not even crave the dessert. Besides, you still have your other half of your meal to enjoy later. Eating healthier will discourage sweet cravings, but if your craving is strong, then be stronger and say no to dessert. If you must cheat, ask others to share dessert. Take a small amount and let it melt in your mouth, again, taking the time to savor the flavor. That one taste just may be enough to satisfy your craving.

Chapter 5

Q2 Exercise

You may like to exercise, or you may not. You may have the motivation, or you may need the motivation. Remove your past experiences and expectations from your mind. Prepare your mind and move your body for your heart, lungs, joints, bones, mind, and overall health and for a great quality of life. Move it for YOU! After all, we only get one body, so why not make it a priority to take care of it, embrace it, nourish it, move it and be in charge. Take ownership.

Our bodies were meant to move, not to keep still.

The easiest and most doable exercise is walking. There are so many gadgets and apps available for you to choose from to hold you accountable. Some phones have apps available that track your steps, floors and miles – however, you need to have your phone with you 24/7. I recommend a fit band, fit watch or a pedometer to wear daily.

The American Heart Association recommends that you walk a minimum of 3,500 steps each day, and that is just active daily steps, steps that you perform throughout the day to function, through work, tasks, chores and your daily life. If you fall short of 3,500 steps, then absolutely read on for assistance and motivation! After all, it is your health.

Use the following Q2 Cardio Walking Zones to help you stay on track while reminding yourself of the importance of moving your body – while encouraging you, whether you like it or not.

Q2 Cardio Walking Zones

Red Zone – under 3,500 steps (Danger Zone)

Yellow Zone – 3,501-7,000 (Burning from your sugar zones)

Green Zone – 7,001-10,000 (Metabolism kicks in and you begin burning from your fat stores)

Purple Zone – 10,001 -13,500 (Determined and absolutely hitting from your fat stores)

Orange Zone – 13,501+ (Warrior)

A person's metabolism will kick in at various times dependent on their lifestyle and other factors as covered in Q2 Metabolism. Start changing your 'no' answers to 'yes' on the metabolism quiz and you will have a more efficient cardio workout.

Walking outside while enjoying nature can encourage a whole host of mental health benefits including positivity, decreased depression, lower stress and improved overall health and well-being. There are so many other outdoor activities that you can truly benefit from. Choose the activities that you like, as you will be more apt to do them and make it a lifestyle. When nature does not comply with your outdoor workouts, then it is time to bring the workout indoors. Don't get caught up on the hamster wheel doing the same thing, the same way and in the same manner. Variety is the key for consistency and results.

Maybe one day you do a full treadmill workout, but another day you bike and envision all the beautiful trails. Switching between different cardio machines during your workout can burn extra calories and challenge your muscles more than trudging along on the same piece of equipment the whole time. Adding a variety of total body exercises along with your cardio will challenge your body and mind.

Q2 Cross-Train Cardio Challenge

Preferably perform cardio training on most days of the week. Keep in mind that moving your body continuously for at least 30 minutes per day and ultimately longer sessions is dependent on what your goal is. Always listen to your body. You Can Do It!

Before you try this cross-train challenge, know your maximum and training heart rate range. It is simple to calculate. Take 220 − minus (your age) = (maximum heart rate). Then take your maximum heart rate (MHR) x multiply .60 (60%) = low/medium-end training heart rate. To calculate your high-end training zone, simply (MHR) x multiply .80 (80%) = high-end training heart rate. Your training heart rate range will be between your low/medium-end training heart and your high-end training heart rate. Keep in mind, your estimated target heart-rate zone is just that − an estimate. Always listen to your body, despite the number.

Ready? Choose your fitness level. Set? Grab your water, heart rate monitor and towel. Go!

	Beginner (2-3x week) *2 sets x 8 repetitions +8-second Isolation	**Intermediate** (3-4x week) *2-3 sets x 12 repetitions +12-second Isolation	**Advanced** (4-5x week) *2-3 sets x 15 repetitions +15-second Isolation
Week 1	15-20 minutes: Walk Cat-Cow* Spinal Balance* 1-legged Knee Lift Balance+ Seated Wall Leg Lifts* Down Dog Stretch+ Jumping Jacks (document the amount achieved)	30-40 minutes: Walk or Run Cat-Cow (6 reps) Spinal Balance and Lifts* 1-legged Knee Lift Balance+ Seated Wall Leg Lifts* Down Dog Stretch+ Jumping Jacks (aim for at least 50 /document amount)	40+ minutes: Walk or Run Cat-Cow (6 reps) Spinal Balance, Lifts and Rotation* 1-legged Knee Lift Balance+ Seated Wall Leg Lifts* Down Dog Stretch+ Jumping Jacks (aim for at least 100 /document amount)
Week 2	20+ minutes: Walk or Bike Cat-Cow* Spinal Balance and Lifts* 1-legged Knee Lift Balance+ Seated Wall Leg Circles* Down Dog Stretch+ Bridge+ Butterfly Crunches* Jumping Jacks (aim for higher reps vs. previous wk)	40+ minutes: Walk, Run, Bike or Elliptical Cat-Cow (4 reps) Spinal Balance, Lifts and Rotation* 1-legged Knee Lift Balance+ Seated Wall Leg Circles* Down Dog Stretch to Plank Down Dog x 4 times Bridge Walks* Butterfly Crunch Reach* Jumping Jacks (aim for higher reps vs. previous wk)	45+ minutes: Walk, Run, Bike or Elliptical Cat-Cow (4 reps) Spinal Balance, Lifts and Rotation* 1-legged Chair Balance+ Seated Wall Leg Circles* Down Dog Stretch to Plank Down Dog x 8 times Bridge Walks* V-Ups x 8 reps Jumping Jacks (aim for higher reps vs. previous wk)

Week 3	25+ minutes: Walk, Bike or Elliptical Cat-Cow (4 reps) Spinal Balance, Lifts and Rotation* 1-legged Knee Lift Balance+ Seated Wall Leg Lift and Circles* Down Dog Stretch to Plank Down Dog x 2 times Bridge Walks* Butterfly Crunch Reach* Modified Burpees* Jumping Jacks (aim for higher reps vs. previous wk)	40+ minutes: Walk, Run, Bike and/or Elliptical - Mix Cat-Cow (4 reps) Spinal Balance, Lifts and Rotation* 1-legged Chair Balance+ Seated Wall Leg Lift and Circles* Down Dog Stretch to Plank Down Dog x 8 times Bridge Walks & Presses* V-Ups x 8 reps Burpees* Jumping Jacks (aim for higher reps vs. previous wk)	45+ minutes: Walk, Run, Bike and/or Elliptical – Mix Cat-Cow (4 reps) Spinal Balance, Lifts and Rotation* 1-legged Chair Balance+ and 1-legged Folding Chair+ Seated Wall Leg Lift and Circles* Down Dog Stretch to Plank to 1-leg Down Dog x8 Bridge Walks & Presses* V-Up to Superman x 8 times Burpees* Jumping Jacks (aim for higher reps vs. previous wk)
Week 4	30+ minutes: Walk, Bike and/or Elliptical – Mix Cat-Cow (4 reps) Spinal Balance, Lifts and Rotation* 1-legged Chair Balance+ Seated Wall Leg Lift and Circles* Down Dog Stretch to Plank Down Dog x 4 Bridge Walks & Glute Lifts* V-Ups* Burpees* Jumping Jacks (aim to beat your highest amount thus far)	40+ minutes: Walk, Run Bike and/or Elliptical –Mix Cat-Cow (4 reps) Spinal Balance, Lifts and Rotation* 1-legged Chair Balance+ and 1-legged Folding Chair+ Seated Wall Leg Lift and Circles* Down Dog Stretch to Plank to 1-leg Down Dog x 8 Bridge Walk, Press, Circles* V-Up to Superman x 8 times Burpees* Jumping Jacks (aim to beat your highest amount thus far)	45+ minutes: Walk, Run, Bike and/or Elliptical – Mix Cat-Cow (4 reps) Spinal Balance, Lifts and Rotation* 1-legged Chair, Folding Chair and Collapse Chair+ Seated Wall Leg Lift and Circles* Down Dog Stretch to Plank to 1-leg Down Dog x 8 Bridge Walk, Press, Circles* V-Up Isolation to roll-over Superman Isolation x 8 reps Burpees* Jumping Jacks (aim to beat your highest amount thus far)

Cat-Cow:

Begin in a 'box' position with shoulders over your wrists and knees in align to your hips. Inhale as you accentuate your spine and let your mid-section drop down so your back caves in. Exhale as you round out your back while you pull your belly button up into your spine.

Spinal Balance:

From a box position, lift your right arm and left leg. Reach your fingers and toes away from the center of your body, as you lengthen and strengthen through your spine to improve your balance. Inhale on the lift and exhale on the down phase. Repeat left arm and right leg.

Modification: Spinal Balance Lift. Lengthen your right arm and left leg – lower the straight arm and leg at the same time where the fingers and toes barely touch the floor. Lift and continue for one set. Repeat left arm and right leg.

Progression: Spinal Balance, Lifts and Rotation. Complete a set of the spinal balance lifts. On the second set, add the rotation. On the lift of the right arm and left leg, rotate the right arm to the right side – opening up the shoulder girdle while you rotate the left leg to the left side – opening up the hip socket. The arm and leg should remain in the air during the rotation set. Repeat left arm and right leg.

1-legged Knee Lift Balance:

Imagine there is a string attached to the top of your head as you lengthen through your spine in a standing position. Pull your belly button toward your spine and find a focal point as you lift your right knee. Keep your eyes on that focal point, breathe and hold your leg during the balance. Repeat on left leg.

Modification: Hold onto the wall with one hand or stand with the back of your body against a wall.

Progression: 1-legged Chair. Begin in a knee lift balance then cross your right ankle over your left thigh. Pull your belly button toward your spine and bend your knees to sit into the stretch - while keeping your torso lengthened. Isolate then switch to the left ankle over your right thigh.

Progression: Folding Chair. From 1-legged chair, place your hands in prayer and slowly bend so that your chest is over the leg and facing the floor. Isolate then repeat on the other side.

Progression: Collapse Chair. From folding chair, place one hand on the floor behind you then the other hand for collapse chair. Challenge yourself by bringing one hand in prayer then the other hand as you go back into folding chair – before lifting up to 1-legged chair. Repeat on the other side.

Seated Wall Leg Lifts:

Begin seated on the floor with your back, head and butt completely against the wall. Relax your shoulders and pull your belly button toward your spine. Lift your right leg then lower to just before your heel touches the floor. Continue to lift and lower for one set. Inhale on the lift, exhale on the down phase. Repeat on left leg.

Modification: Assist the movement of your leg by supporting your leg with your hands.

Progression: Seated Wall Leg Circles. Lift the right leg and keep the leg up as you complete a set of small circles clockwise then counterclockwise. Repeat on the left leg. Don't hold onto the floor for support.

Down Dog Stretch:

From an upside down 'V' position, let your head hang through your arms lengthening through your neck - spiral your elbows toward your ears. Pull your rib cage toward your hips, pull your heels toward the earth, and if your heels touch, then you are too close together – you want to get that stretchy pulling feeling on the back of your legs.

Modification: Place your hands on a low chair instead of the floor.

Plank:

Begin on your hands and feet in a plank position with the hands below the shoulders. Find a focus point on the floor, keep your cervical spine (neck) in alignment to the rest of the spine. Lengthen through your neck as you pull your shoulders away from your ears. Maintain a strong core by pulling your belly button toward your spine. Don't let your hips and butt sag or raise up - keep your butt and hips in alignment.

Modification: Lower onto your knees as you keep your weight forward and maintain strength and alignment in your core.

Progression: Down Dog Stretch to Plank Down Dog. Begin in down dog stretch then transition to plank and back to down dog. Repeat.

Progression: Down Dog Stretch to Plank to 1-leg Down Dog. Begin in down dog stretch then transition to plank as you move to down dog, lift and lengthen your right leg up toward the ceiling. Move to plank then lift and lengthen your left leg up. Continue alternating.

Bridge:

From a lying position, bend your knees in alignment to your ankles and with your feet shoulder width apart. Raise your hips as you relax your head, neck and shoulders. Imagine strings are attached to your hips as you lift and lengthen as high as your body will allow you to. Breathe as you hold the position.

Progression: Bridge Walks. Maintain your strong bridge position and lift your right extended leg to the ceiling for a 1-legged bridge. Place the foot down and switch to the left leg. Continue alternating for a full set of bridge walks.

Progression: Bridge Presses. Begin in a one-legged bridge and as you lengthen the leg up, slowly lower the butt slightly and press the leg up again. Continue to press for one set then switch to the other side.

Progression: Bridge Circles. After a set of bridge presses, immediately progress to circles on the same leg. Keep the leg up and make small controlled circles with your leg clockwise for one set then counter clockwise for one set. Think about moving your leg with your lower abs and not your leg. Maintain the height of your hips. Repeat on the other side.

Butterfly Crunches:

Lie on your back with your legs in a butterfly position. Pull your belly button toward the spine. With  your abdominal muscles – lift your head, neck and shoulders while you reach your fingers through your legs. Keep your head still and lower your head to right before it touches the floor – for one set. Exhale on the lift.

Modification: Place your hands behind your neck for cervical support.

V-Ups:

Lie on your back, pull your belly button toward your spine. Inhale as you lift the upper and lower part of the body at the same time. Only lift as high as your body will allow you to – then exhale as you slowly lower down at the same time.

Modification: On the lift, place your elbows on the floor and hold the back of your legs as you use assistance to lift into and lower from a lower 'V'.

Superman:

Lie on the floor with your arms and legs extended and lengthened. Pull your belly button up toward  your spine to support your lower back. Lift the arms and legs at the same time as you reach your fingers and toes away from the center of your body. Hold the isolation as you breathe.

Progression: V-Ups to roll-over Superman. Execute one V-up then roll to the right onto the stomach. Execute one superman. Roll back. Repeat alternating rolling to the right then the left.

Progression: Isolate the V-up and superman for 4, 8 or 12 counts.

Jumping Jacks:

Stand with your feet together then jump your feet open as you clap your hands overhead. Bring your arms down as you jump your feet back together. Repeat.

Modification: In place of jumping, side step one foot out at a time.

Burpees:

From a standing position, bend at your knees as you touch the floor. Jump your feet back into a plank position. Jump your feet back in so that you are touching the floor and your knees are bent. Stand. Repeat.

Modification: Walk your feet back as opposed to jumping. To modify further, place your hands on a bench or table in place of the floor.

Progression: Jump up when completing the exercise. To progress further, execute a plank jumping jack from a plank position before coming back up.

The exercises should be done in proper form for optimal benefits and safety. Connect your body and mind during your practice. For instance, Down Dog is not just an upside down 'V' – get into position and let your head hang through your arms lengthening through your neck - spiral your elbows toward your ears. Pull your rib cage toward your hips, pull your heels toward the earth, and if your heels touch, then you are too close together – you want to get that stretchy pulling feeling on the back of your legs. Let the blood pool to the brain to improve mental acuity and clarity. Wow! That was a lot! If you are going to put the time in to a workout, then you might as well do it with mind-body connection. Mind-body connection really matters! Think about it or try it, go into your upside down 'V' – what does the exercise mean? What is the goal of the exercise? How do you breathe? Need assistance on verbal and visual instruction of exercises?

Log onto www.Q2Fit.com or www.youniquelifelongfitness.com to register for this challenge and for all future challenges. Be a part of the Q2 community and you will receive video exercise instructions, flash challenges with prizes, a weekly food plan, additional recipes and food prep, motivation and accountability.

Q2 No Excuse '300' Workout

The more muscle you have, the more fat you will burn, even at rest. You don't have to have equipment to build strong muscles – YOU are the equipment! Use your own body weight for the following 'no excuse' workout. That's right, all fitness levels can do this work out and the best thing is you can do it anywhere, even in a hotel room when travelling or on vacation.

The '300' consists of squats, push-ups and crunches by executing ten squats, ten push-ups and ten crunches in that order ten times for a total of 300. Seem far-fetched? Or easy? No worries - listen to your body or challenge yourself. This workout has you covered - working the upper body, lower body and core with a cardio component from moving without delay from one exercise to another.

Follow the modifications or progression of each exercise:

Execution of Squats: Stand shoulder width apart. Be aware of knees and pretend like you are sitting in a chair (or actually have a chair behind you and barely touch your butt on the chair). Make sure that your knees do not go past your toes and pull your belly button toward your spine on the way down while squeezing your butt on the way up.

Execution of Push Ups: Get into a plank position and lower your body toward the ground then push back up. Make sure that your core is strong by pulling your belly button up toward your spine and that your elbows are in a straight line over your wrists when you come down into a push up. Bring it down for two counts, then push up for two counts.

Modify by executing the push-ups on your knees. If you do this, make sure that you bring your body weight forward and your butt is not up in the air. If this is still hard for you or if you have shoulder/wrist issues, you can still do it! Put your hands on a bench, desk table or something supportive. Bring your chest down toward the support system then push back up. Always listen to your body and change the range of motion if necessary. If this is still challenging for you, execute the push up by placing your hands on a wall while placing your feet back as far as you feel comfortable. Bend your elbows and bring your body weight forward toward the wall, then push back. Again, make sure that your elbows are aligned with your wrists.

Execution of Reverse Crunches: Lie on your back, bend your knees and lift your legs up so your knees are over your hips. Place your arms and hands on the floor next to your body. Keep your head, neck and shoulders relaxed on the floor while you slowly lift your butt up off of the floor as your knees go toward your chest. Finish by slowly lowering your butt back down by using the power of your abs. Nice and slow.

Progression of reverse crunches: Place your arms over your head, next to your ears, while lifting and lowering your butt slowly for muscle isolation and control in the abdominals. If you find that you are lowering your body down too fast, then switch to arms along the body for support before moving to the progression.

Before you know it, you have accomplished 100 squats, 100 push-ups and 100 crunches. The next step in your accomplishment is to challenge yourself for the next session. Didn't quite make it to all ten sets? No worries. Challenge yourself to do one or more sets the next time and build up each time until you meet the goal of '300'!

Q2 Resistance Matters

Resistance training is one of the best things you can do if you would like to have a body with confidence – a stronger and tighter body. Resistance training is also known as strength training or weight training, which involves activities that use weights, machines, various equipment and even your own body weight. Whatever your preference and availability are is the best choice for you as they all work your muscles.

Strength training is quite often associated with body builders who work hard at increasing muscle size. If this is your goal, then your exertion of reps with heavier weights will need to increase with the use of free weights and weight machines.

The resistance training that I am referring to will basically build and tone the muscles in order to give your body a better look and to make you feel better. Strength training is extremely important to seniors who wish to maintain mobility. I recommend that seniors use light to moderate intensity seated machine training and the use of resistance tubing.

The key to a resistance training program at least three times a week is to put action into it. Make an appointment with yourself. Move on your lunch hour. Why? Many people have sedentary jobs which can cause your body to adapt by allowing your muscles to shrink or atrophy. The following are vital benefits of resistance training:

– **Reduced Body Fat**

  It is a proven fact that muscle burns more calories at rest than fat. Not only will resistance training build fat burning muscles, but fat is also being burned as you work out. Your muscle tone will improve as your fat reduces, and the shape of your body will improve.

– **Increased Bone Mineral**

Bone density is constantly remodeling, meaning the tissues break down at the same time they build up. The peak rebuilding time is during puberty. However, as a person ages, your bone density changes, due to activity and hormone level changes. This is especially a problem for post-menopausal women whose changing hormones can rob the bone mass of minerals. Resistance training can also help prevent osteoporosis, which is thinning of the bone mass and can cause bones to become brittle and more susceptible to breakage.

– **Increased Strength**

Developing strength in the muscles and bones will improve your bone density and BMI – body mass index – the ratio of muscle and fat.

– **Improved Mobility**

Our bodies were made to move. Resistance training throughout your life will improve your health and reduce the risks of aging. Stay independent, without needing to rely on other people to do those once simple things. A weak body is much more prone and at risk for injury and the cause of falls and accidents. Continue to move as our bodies were intended to do.

– **Increased Range of Activities**

When your body is strong enough to carry your own weight, then you will also have the capability of doing more activities. You will also feel energized and more apt to live a more active lifestyle.

- **Improve Heart and Overall Health**

  Regular resistance training can result in a lowered heart rate, lowered blood pressure and improved overall health. The risk of heart disease, injury and sickness is reduced to a considerable extent.

Resistance training should always be performed properly. Seek a fitness professional for guidance as it requires commitment and consistency. If training is performed incorrectly it can result in injury. The key to starting any program is to begin slow, listen to your body to back off or push yourself a little more. Mind-muscle connection will assist in doing the exercise correctly and effectively. As your body condition improves, you may move on to more challenging tasks.

Q2 Flexibility Matters

Your flexibility decreases as you age and, of course, with inactivity. I hear time and time again, I can't do Yoga because I am not flexible. You don't have to be flexible to practice Yoga, as Yoga will make you more flexible. The practice of Yoga is only one way you can increase your flexibility, and there are various types of stretching that can suit your needs. However, when you stretch, incorporate the techniques of Yoga by breathing through the stretch and maintaining the awareness of your ability, while honoring what struggles your body may encounter as you connect mind and body to their full potential, and to the best safe stretch.

Static Stretching is the traditional method of stretching where you hold the stretch for 20-30 seconds, being mindful that the initiation of the stretch has the same benefit of the whole stretch, if not more. For instance, if you perform a forward bend stretch (reach for your toes), think about the stretch first. If you were to come down by bending your waist then you are stretching out of shortened back and hamstring muscles. Rethink the stretch and lengthen your arms overhead, reaching out of your shoulders, out of your hips, and then bend slowly halfway down as you continue to come forward into the stretch. Hold the stretch for 20-30 seconds as you reach your fingers toward your toes without bouncing. Always perform the same stretch 2-3 times for optimal stimulation, movement and performance.

Dynamic stretching is considered an active stretch because the muscle is contracting and relaxing as in squats and lunges, yet also focuses on speed and taking the muscle through its range of motion, as in arm circles. This type of stretching is favorable, but not limited to those that are preparing for a hard training session. Keep in mind that even the advanced exerciser can risk injury on any given day. Always perform 2-3 minutes of movement to warm up the body prior to dynamic stretching.

A passive stretch or assisted stretching is done with the help of equipment or another person. This type of stretching will allow your muscles to stretch beyond your own initial ability, yet make sure that you are listening to your body's abilities. An assisted strap stretch can increase your range of motion of the stretch. For instance, in a hamstring stretch, when lying on the floor, lift one leg up while lengthening it and assist the stretch with your hands wrapped around your leg to go into the stretch a little deeper. Then try that same stretch but wrap a strap under your foot and as you raise the leg, lengthen and gently pull the strap to ease you into the stretch even further. This same stretch, along with many other stretches, can be assisted by another person, but always make sure that you seek help from a knowledgeable fitness professional.

Not sure why flexibility matters? Check out the following reasons and rethink your plan:

- **Releases stress**

  Yes! Who doesn't want to release stress? Stretching increases the blood flow to your muscles and brain where it can effectively reduce the muscle tension and even improve your mood.

- **Eases back pain**

  There is a rising prevalence of chronic back pain and one that can be avoided with proper stretching techniques. Think of the core of your body as the stem of a flower. That stem needs to be strong, without weakness, so that the flower can survive. Adding stretches along with resistance training for your back and abs can create a strong, invulnerable core.

- **Therapeutic**

  Improve your sleep by light stretching before bed. Stretching can also be therapeutic during those leg cramps or muscle aches.

- **Strengthens your muscles**

  Stretching should not replace your strength training routine, but static stretching does work your muscles on a lower scale of strength training. The two combined are a powerful team.

- **Joint health**

  When you stretch, you move your joints in a full range of motion and increase the flexibility in your tendons, which connect your muscles to the bones.

- **Improved muscle control and exercise form**

  Warm, stretched and loose muscles are necessary to prepare your muscles for exercise and to achieve good form. In turn, your workouts will be much more effective while having more muscle control.

— **Prevents injuries**

Tightened muscles are vulnerable and are at risk of injuries or other health issues. Injuries can be prevented through proper and safe stretching.

The practice of Yoga will reap the same benefits and enhance other positive effects on the body, mind and overall being. Yoga provides an opportunity to connect mind, body and spirit with improved mental acuity, balance, mindfulness, personal health and self-awareness. Yoga may even alleviate various medical symptoms, as certain poses and movements help stimulate not only your muscles, but also your internal organs.

Yes, flexibility matters!

Add some flexibility in your life
and create a positive effect on your workouts,
everyday chores, your overall health and quality of life.

Q2 Reprogram YOUR Exercise Attitude

We make hair and dental appointments for ourselves, and yet we forget to take our mental health and physical well-being into account. What is your exercise attitude? Many of us associate exercise with discomfort, and it's that emotional connection that keeps us inactive or skipping our workouts. When you like something, you find time to do it. You rarely hear someone say that they don't have time to do something that they enjoy, because they will find the time.

You can reprogram your exercise attitude by, first and foremost, finding your why. Get out of your comfort zone and consider group training. A group can provide balance and emotional support and being a member of a group will improve your confidence and fulfill your sense of accomplishment. Some people shy away from group exercise because they think, "What if everyone is watching me?" Rid yourself of the negative thinking, because this simply is not the case.

Exercise is a mind-body connection and is best practiced with the interpretation of exercise as being non-judgmental. By connecting body and mind during exercise, you will experience an awareness that will aid in effectiveness of the workout. The result? A positive experience that will reprogram your attitude and re-energize your body and your mind.

You can't expect to prevent negative feelings altogether. And you can't expect to experience positive feelings all the time . . . The Law of Emotional Choice directs us to acknowledge our feelings but also to refuse to get stuck in the negative ones.

Chapter 6

Q2 Mind Matters

The psychology of holistic fitness is that you must accept who you are and how you feel inside. We will learn to 'let go' of any emotional, physical or spiritual pain or heaviness to truly connect body and mind. The mind-body connection, in its simplest definition, is a relationship between the brain and the body. We all inherently know that the two coexist, sometimes in harmony with each other and sometimes in struggle with each other. The mind-body connection is an internal balance that encourages your sense of well-being. Having the awareness of how your body and mind interact is an important first step in understanding this connection. Observe yourself, listen to yourself, monitor yourself. Maybe you will notice that you tend to get headaches on days you don't eat enough, eat too much or haven't had enough water. Notice times that you tend to hold your breath. It may not be just during the last two biceps or abdominal crunches. It may be when you are at work, driving and running late, or even in an emotionally heavy conversation.

Having an awareness of how your mind and body interact is a starting point. From there, practice balance. Practice making small changes in areas that are not serving your overall sense of well-being. If you find yourself swinging from one extreme to another in your life's pendulum, you also know the feelings of frustration and loss of control that follow. For example, if you can't get to those 45-minute cardio sessions you planned, accept the 30-minute session or even the 15-minute session that you can do. This is balance. Any activity or even a moment of time that gives you opportunity to self-reflect, to grow, to try to breathe, or simply to be is balance. Yoga has become very popular, and while many people begin yoga as a fitness alternative, they are hooked by the relaxation and spiritual aspects. Religion also offers many people a sense of balance. Positive relationships with others, reading, self-pampering, healthy exercise and eating, turning off the cell phones and technological devices are just a few other ways to seek balance.

A mind-body connection is something to be attained, and through practice you will discover your healthy connection!

A Higher Conscious Living

The mind and how we think is very complicated, but it can be simplified as being comprised of the conscious and subconscious. The conscious mind is the thoughts and things that come to your awareness. The subconscious mind is the activity of the brain you are not aware of. It controls and processes a large amount of information you receive, and it runs the body.

For success in any endeavor, the subconscious mind must be in tune with your conscious desires. It is the role of the subconscious that will determine the outcome. If the conscious mind determined success, then any goal you said you wanted to achieve you would easily attain, provided you knew how. This is not the case.

The subconscious is where your previous experiences and beliefs are held. These can be thought of as the writing on the wall of your mind. Whenever you try and act consciously, the subconscious first checks with the writing inside the mind to see that this is something you really want to do. For example, if you thought, "I am going to jump in the fire," the subconscious would check with what it has written down in your mind about fire and influence your decision. This is obviously vital in this example, and the writing in your mind on this subject is clear, "Fire burns, burns hurt . . . do not jump in."

However, what happens when a more neutral thought occurs that has conflicting writing on the wall? For example, if you said, "I want to lose ten pounds of fat," the subconscious writing on the wall may read, "You need to do this, you will feel great,", but at the same time, there may also be thoughts saying, "You cannot lose weight," beliefs saying, "You will become unpopular among your friends at work" and memories saying, "Fit people are arrogant" and "You don't deserve to be fit." These would all conflict with the conscious, and ultimately, these thoughts, beliefs and memories would determine your behavior.

There are many reasons why you may feel an endless amount of ways, but they will mostly stem from events in the past. Perhaps memories of being made fun of in your youth or a life-changing event like a divorce or the loss of a loved one. Sometimes people may be punishing themselves for something they did. Another common factor is that people find an emotional comfort, like in food or with bad habits like cigarettes, which causes them to gain weight and continue smoking. To try to take this away from them or limit them, you take away their emotional support.

Practice higher conscious living. It is living each day in full awareness of yourself in the moment. It is living free of self-criticism and judgement.

It is living with your body and mind being in the right relationship with one another, as opposed to being in war with each other, as is often the case with diets, extreme exercise regimens, negative and unsupportive surroundings, and even self-help books. Seriously, self-help implies that something is wrong with you. You are in some way broken and need fixing. It implies you are not good enough the way that you are. I propose that you are good enough and complete exactly as you are. You can realize it through higher conscious living. Here's how:

1. **Create a Quiet Moment**. To live in the moment, you have to feel what moment is for yourself. Start by creating a quiet moment. Sit or lay down. Be comfortable. Be quiet, still and undisturbed. Set aside twenty minutes. If this is a challenge, look at your roles and responsibilities and set boundaries. Go no further until you have created this quiet moment. If your life is so pressed that you don't have twenty minutes of quiet to yourself, you need rest. Take it.

2. **Breathe**. As cliché as it sounds, you need to breathe. Breathe fully. Count 10 breaths. Inhale-exhale equals one breath. Notice where in your body you feel the breath the most. For example, you may be most aware of your breathing in your chest, nostrils, throat, or abdomen. This is your anchor point. Focus on this point as you breathe.

3. **Roaming**. Let your mind roam for a while. It is difficult to sit still and meditate. The brain is always on and scrolling through the 'to do' lists and agenda – this is why twenty minutes is essentials for starters. The first 5-10 minutes is the brain unleashing itself, bombarding you with reminders and instant messages. This is also the time when the body fidgets and impatience bubbles. This is normal. Stay with it. After this roaming period, the brain eventually does slow down and shift gears to a place you can be comfortable

in. You are fully conscious, alert and aware of your surrounding but not hyper or agitated.

4. **Set an Intention**. Intentions are a desire from within. It is an aim that guides action. It is not a goal or an outcome. Rather it is planting of a small seed and leaving the rest alone. It is faith, hope and love realized. After your brain has roamed for a while, ask yourself what you desire from within. What do you need to feel in your heart and in your spirit? What is your wish?

5. **Meditate on your Intention**. Continue to breathe and focus on your intention. Repeating your intention or making it your mantra is helpful. By this point, other thoughts may interrupt again. Again, this is normal. Continue to focus on your breathing, your intention. The brain meditates on the bell-curve, in cycles, much like an ocean wave. The first 5-10 minutes is the preparation, the noise, or constant brain chatter. The next five minutes or so is the quieting and the open window for setting intentions and meditating. The remaining five minutes is a re-surfacing of brain chatter letting you know you are about done.

6. **Let it Be.** Once you've breathed, set an intention, and meditated upon it, let it be. Rest your body for five minutes before getting up. Lying on your left side is best for circulation and restoration. Initially you may need to use a timer for twenty minutes, in case you fall asleep or continually wonder how much time has passed.

7. **Practice**. Create a quiet moment for yourself for twenty minutes each day and meditate on your intention. Be patient and be consistent. It is the consistent practice of coming home to yourself and your deepest desires that allow you to live from a higher consciousness. You will notice you react differently to others and

to life's little annoyances. You will live in your body in a way that is healthy and balanced. You will live in each moment feeling fulfilled.

Breathing & Relaxation Techniques

The way you breathe affects your whole body. Full, deep breathing is a good way to reduce tension, feel relaxed and reduce stress. There are several breathing techniques that you may want to consider. After all, without breath, there is no life. Breathing techniques have proven to help reduce tension and stress, calm anxiety, clear your thoughts, help with circulation and improve your overall health and well-being. Take a few minutes a day to concentrate on your breathing. Is it heavy? Is it fast? Or is fluid and calm? It may change within the day dependent on your life happenings. Stress, poor posture, snug clothes and habit are some of the reasons that keep us from breathing properly. We end up using our chest muscles instead of our abdomen. Belly breathing, also called diaphragmatic breathing, is a simple deep breathing technique that teaches you how to use your diaphragm, a sheet of muscle at the bottom of our lungs and the most important muscle for breathing. The goal should be to breathe this way all of the time. Take notice and use the following breathing techniques for a better quality of life.

First, calm your mind. Sit in a chair with your legs uncrossed, stand or preferably lie on your back. Close your eyes. Forget about your day, your errands, your tasks, your responsibilities. Shut out any outside noises and turn off your inside voices. Don't force it. Let go of any physical, emotional, spiritual pain or heaviness. Any negative feelings, thoughts and energy are far away from your mind, body and spirit and all the positive energy is restored within. With a clear mind and a relaxed physical body, open up your heart to restore your spiritual body. Place all of the colors of a rainbow within side of your heart; Red for

Love, Green for Peace, Yellow for Happiness, Orange for Courage, Blue for Serenity and Purple for Vitality. Continue to relax, connect and calm as we come into awareness of your posture and being.

Connect with your posture. Proper posture gets air into your lungs and helps energy flow through your body. Sit or lie straight, and imagine a string is attached to the top of your head, lifting and lengthening you. You should feel the area between your chest and your navel lengthen. As you try to improve your posture, you may find your muscles tensing up, especially around the abdomen. Consciously try to release any tension from your body. With a calm and connected mind and body, you are ready to breathe.

Breathe in through your nose. Bring the breath into your throat then slowly push it down into your lungs. Feel your chest rise. Continue to push the breath down into the pit of your stomach. Feel your stomach rise. Hold the breath in your stomach for a moment then push the breath up out of your stomach as your stomach deflates. Continue to slowly push the breath up and out of your lungs as your chest deflates. Then slowly push the breath out of the throat and back out of your nose. I prefer using the nose for both the inhale and exhale when practicing relaxation breathing and in the practice of Yoga. However, I use the nose for the inhale and the mouth on the exhalation when practicing Pilates as the force of breath from the mouth is much more effective with this type of exercise. There is no right or wrong. This is your experience, your time to breathe, your time to connect. Honor what your body will and will not allow you to do. Shut out any judgements. Release any emotion. Repeat this sequence a few more times. You will be amazed at how much more you can accomplish within the day and how you deal with your daily tasks and responsibilities.

Roll breathing is another technique. The object of roll breathing is to develop full use of your lungs and get in touch with the rhythm of your breathing. It can be practiced in any position, but it is best to learn it lying on your back with your knees bent. Place your left hand on your abdomen and your right hand on your chest. Notice how your hands move as you breathe in and out. Practice filling your lower lungs by breathing so that your left hand goes up on the inhalation and your right hand remains still. When you have filled and emptied your lower lungs eight to ten times, add the second step to your breathing. Inhale first into your lower lungs as before, and then continue inhaling into your upper chest. As you do so, raise your right hand and your left hand will fall a little as your abdomen falls. Exhale slowly through your mouth. Listen to your breath leaving your body as your left hand, and then your right hand, fall. As you exhale, feel the tension leaving your body as you become more and more relaxed. Practice breathing in and out in this manner for three to five minutes. Notice that the movement of your abdomen and chest is like rolling waves rising and falling in a rhythmic motion.

Practice morning breathing before you get out of bed. Pull your knees toward your chest and hug yourself. Take a long deep breathe to release any tension from your mid-section; back and abs. Then take another long deep breath as you stretch and lengthen your body before getting out of bed to relieve muscle stiffness and clear clogged breathing passages. Use your breath throughout the day to relieve any tension, clear your mind and relax your body. From a standing position, inhale and lift your arms up and overhead and reach your fingers away from the center of your body. Stretch out of your hips, out of your shoulders. Pull your belly button to your spine to support your lower back then slowly bend forward from the waist with your knees slightly bent. Let the top of your head and arms dangle toward the floor and exhale. As you inhale slowly and deeply, return to a standing position by rolling up slowly one vertebra at a time, lifting and stacking your head up on top last. Hold your breath for just a few seconds in this standing position then exhale again slowly as you return to the original standing position.

Distractions and overwhelming events can create neck tension due to your subconscious breath. Bring your breath into awareness and clear your mind with neck rolls. Let your chin fall naturally to your chest, inhale and roll your head up and to the right as you look over your shoulder. Then exhale while dropping your chin toward your armpit and rolling your chin back to the chest. Inhale and roll your head up and to the left as you look over your shoulder. Then exhale while dropping your chin toward your left armpit and then rolling your chin back to the chest. Repeat three to four times, moving slowly. Don't make this movement mechanical, just relax and roll.

Practice a variety of breathing techniques to experience how you are like an amazing machine – capable of releasing, connecting and rejuvenating – by using the breathing technique that fits your needs.

Q2

Chapter 7

Be Comfortable in YOUR Skin

Q2 Body Image

Body image is simply YOUR perception of how you look. It is how you feel about your appearance. Not what everyone else thinks how your body should look, nor do they know how you feel. Overall body image can be intimidating due to the high-profile demands on looks in our society today. The key is to feel comfortable in your own skin. We are all made differently and different we shall be – find your beautiful and be your own kind of beautiful. Look at yourself in the mirror and what do you see? A positive body image yields self-confidence, happiness and high self-esteem. A negative or distorted body image can yield insecurity, frustration, unhappiness and self-loathing. Others tend to view us more realistically and objectively while we tend to view ourselves through our own cloudy mind's eye. We are indeed our own worst critics. We are quick to see the fat, the wrinkles, and the weaknesses, while barely noticing the beauty, the vessel and the strengths.

Positive body image is key to healthy living and a healthy outlook. It is especially important for anyone trying to create change in life, whether it is weight loss, a new job or a new relationship. If you find that you often give yourself negative self-talk, or that you make critical judgements of yourself on a regular basis, you must stop it! Right now! Your body can hear you, and it remembers every criticism and complaint your brain makes. For every negative mental statement made, it takes many positive statements to repair it. So, begin to take note of how you talk to yourself internally. What kind of messages do you feed yourself? How do you see yourself? Can you find positive qualities about your body? Embrace your body and accept the things that you cannot change!

Use the following journal. Challenge yourself to do this for 28 days. It is very simple and can be quite revealing about your own body image truth.

Seeking Sunday: Today I felt _____ about myself and _____ about my body.

Motivational Monday: Today I liked _____ about myself and _____ about my body.

Topic Tuesday: Today I will journal - feelings about myself, my life and my goals.

Wellness Wednesday: Take 20 minutes to self-reflect or meditate. How did this make me feel?

Thankful Thursday: Today I am thankful for _____.

Forget Friday: Today I will forget any negative feelings and state a positive feeling about myself.

Stop Saturday: Stop and smell the roses – as cliché as it may sound – look around, look at you, look in the mirror and smile. You are so blessed, beautiful and unstoppable from doing anything and being anything. Can you feel the beauty inside? Do you see the beauty of your body?

Practice daily healing and affirmation. Find a picture of yourself that you love. Keep that picture near and dear to you – as you are the same – one – let the unity of the beauty within yourself shine. You will then be one step closer to seeing the beauty of your shell and feeling comfortable in your own skin.

Q2 Tips to Look and Feel Your Personal Best

Do you have a special event that you are attending and would like to feel energized and rested - without the bloating? Well, you can! Increase your workouts the week before the event; cardio, so you feel light and lean, and resistance with higher repetitions and lighter weights to help tighten the skin by squeezing the water out.

Follow these simple tips and tricks forty-eight hours before your special event:

- Eliminate carbonated drinks and alcohol.
- Drink an extra 16 ounces of water a day (Beyond the half your body weight in ounces)
- Drink your daily water with lemons and/or limes to naturally detoxify your kidneys.
- Avoid gum chewing and drinking out of a straw. The extra air can cause bloat.
- Eliminate whites; white sugar, white flour, hydrogenated oil, high fructose corn syrup.
- Eliminate dairy and gluten as it can cause bloat.
- Eat oatmeal or quinoa. These two complex carbohydrates will provide fiber without the bloat.

It also releases slow sugar to help lower your glycemic index.

- Eat colorful! Small portions throughout the day, preferably 5-6 times. Choose a protein/grain with a vegetable 4 times and fruit 1-2 times with seeds, nuts or protein.

- Eat green, but limit gassy cruciferous vegetables like kale, cauliflower, broccoli and Brussels sprouts.

- Limit bean intake as it can cause gas and bloat.

- Eliminate the use of sugar substitutes and sugar alcohol.

- Make sure you eat enough throughout the day otherwise you may end up extremely hungry, which can cause you to eat more than you need and create cravings.

- If you are hungry at night, try drinking hot tea. De-caffeinated green tea, white tea, peppermint, ginger and chamomile are some better choices, and filled with antioxidants.

- Don't add additional salt to food.

- Eliminate sodium the day before your event. Choose a banana for your fruit because the potassium will help eliminate sodium in your body.

- Get outdoors with some natural sunlight.

- Get at least 7 ½ hours of sleep. One REM (rapid eye movement) session is 90 minutes. 7 ½ hours or 9 hours will put you at the end of a full restful REM session.

- Listen to your body. Push it, but don't overdo it. Rest extra if needed.

- Stretch and practice relaxation techniques.

- The mind, body and spirit are very much connected. Push any negative thoughts or energy far, far away. Keep positive vibes with you always to attract positivity in your life and well-being.

- Learn to love yourself and your body and you will carry yourself with an inspiring and joyful confidence.
- Pamper yourself. Cherish your body. It is the shell for our soul. If you feel better on the outside, then you will feel better on the inside.
- YOU CAN DO IT!

Chapter 8

Q2 Prep Rally

Through the years of training, I have heard from my clients – "I don't have time" "I don't like to cook" "I don't know how to cook" or "It's easier to order out." You can believe in these excuses or you can do something about it. It was a pivotal time in my career when I decided to do something about it – combining my passion for cooking and teaching my clients hands-on on how to eat healthy. I invited my clients to My Home Kitchen to show them the simplicity of cooking and food prep. They were amazed at how doable the food prep and recipes were, how enjoyable it was to prepare, and how the delicious fresh flavors happily bounced in their mouths.

They were so inspired and eager to apply healthy cooking into their daily lives. In turn, they encouraged me to teach a monthly healthy cooking class and ultimately, achieve the completion of this book. I will be forever grateful.

Maximize Food Prep for Optimal Healthy Living

As I taught my monthly cooking classes, I realized that there is so much more to share – vital tips for optimal healthy living. For instance, not only fueling your body with many wonderful colors of fruits and vegetables, but also sharing how to prepare them. I am not talking about how to use them in recipes quite yet, since there is a vital step when bringing them into your kitchen – how to wash them.

Have you ever heard of the dirty dozen? They are the top twelve fruits and vegetables that contain pesticides, and that is just the top twelve. There may be a residue of chemicals and pesticides as farmers' crops are filled with them nowadays. Even if you eat organic, do you know if they were packaged or delivered near chemical-laden foods, how they were processed or how many bugs, crawled, landed and even pooped on the produce? Exactly! After mortifying my class participants, which was not my intent, they were interested to know the process that I used. The most natural way to deep clean your produce is with distilled white vinegar or apple cider vinegar. Neither will leave an aftertaste on your food but will cleanse it and even preserve it for longer use. Raspberries always impress me the most – the sometimes dingy coloring, the seeds and the secret holes in them – after cleaning with vinegar, they are so succulent, the most vibrant red as they should be, the unwanted dead seeds naturally fall off and the holes are free and clear of any creatures or chemicals.

How to wash fruits and vegetables is simple – soak your produce in a large bowl of water with a tablespoon of white or apple cider vinegar for 5 minutes. Then rinse with cold water completely in a colander. Drain, eat, prepare or store away for later. If I happen to pick up a small carton of berries, I will soak them in a teaspoon of vinegar and water. There is no formula for measurements that I am aware of, but there is a taste, preservation and comfort that I have experienced.

I shared this information with my niece via phone and later found out that she did this washing process, but she was putting the produce right in the kitchen sink. No bowl, no colander, but in the sink – the sink where there are a multitude of germs lurking. Yikes! Please do not use the basin of your kitchen sink to wash your food – always use precaution and safe sanitary methods.

Okay, so now you are thinking you are spending more time with food prep. Yes, you may, but this is vital to your health. This is what you are putting into your body.

Here are some more Q2 tips and food for thought:

- Do you cook with aluminum foil? Don't let the aluminum foil touch your food while cooking as the heat can release chemicals into your food.

- Minimize use of plastic. Keep plastic food containers away from heat as heat tends to promote the leaching of chemicals – even in safer types of plastics.

- Nix canned goods that are not BPA-free. Epoxy resins may be used to line aluminum cans and may be used in your canned soups or veggies. This is another reason to eat fresh and make your own pasta sauce with fresh tomatoes, delicious home-made soups and to visit your fresh produce market. There are certain foods that are listed in the Q2 recipes that are canned, however I encourage you to use BPA-free canned goods.

- Refrigerate your food within a timely manner. Bacteria can grow on food within two hours, especially on high-risk foods such as meat, poultry, fish, eggs and dairy products.

- Do not thaw food on the counter. If you eat fresh, then you will not have to worry about thawing. If you do thaw, keep in mind that harmful germs can multiply extremely rapidly at room temperature, making your food unsafe to eat. To thaw food safely, let it defrost in the refrigerator or run it under cold water.

- Marinate and marinade (M2) safely. Always marinate in the refrigerator where it can safely soak up the flavor. Using the marinade for sauces can spread germs, but you can boil it to make it safe and use again. Otherwise, discard immediately.

- Use different utensils and plates from raw to cooked meat, poultry and fish and be careful not to handle other foods with the utensils and plates from your raw foods.

- Don't wash your meat, poultry or fish. Just cook them. Washing them can spread bacteria to your sink, countertops and other surfaces in your kitchen.

- Wash your hands. Run your hands under sudsy soap – preferably chemical and paraben free – before handling food, between food prep and afterward.

Now let's talk cookware. Yes, cookware. Did you know that healthier cookware is almost as important as the quality of food that you put in it? Replace your non-stick pans and your aluminum cookware and bakeware. Non-stick pans cans release a toxic gas when they are heated above 500 degrees. Aluminum cookware and bakeware can release small amounts of metal in the body, especially when acidic foods are cooked in them. Both non-stick and aluminum can cause a whole host of health problems, inability to lose weight and disrupted metabolism due to foreign and toxic products released into the human body.

Cast iron and carbon steel cookware can withstand the heat and are a healthier choice. If you are using acidic foods such as tomatoes, lemons or vinegar, however, it can give your food a metallic taste. Enameled cast iron may be the best choice for all foods, including acidic food, as it is so diverse that it can go from stovetop to right into the oven. Stainless steel is also healthier if it is 18/10 stainless steel either with a core of aluminum or copper. Cooking directly on aluminum or copper is unhealthy, but the combination of the two or by itself provides excellent heat conductivity.

Follow the Q2 tip for getting the hard-to-get-off food from your cookware and bakeware. Squeeze dishwashing detergent in the cookware or bakeware and fill with water, just above the mess. Either reheat on the cooktop if it was used on the cooktop or reheat it in the heated oven. Bring to a boil on the cooktop, then use a soft spatula or non-abrasive cleaning brush to release the food from the bottom and sides. Use the same protocol for the ovenware, let the heat from the oven release the remnants for at least ten minutes. Voila! A healthier way to eat while minimizing your clean up time!

Grocery Store Tips

It's time to fill your kitchen with healthy foods so they are easily accessible for healthy whole snacks and to create delicious healthy meals. The grocery store can seem overwhelming and can be distracting with the displays and end caps reeling you in. Be brave. Make a list, stay focused and fill your cart with what you came to buy. I tell clients to shop mainly the perimeter of the store in the produce department, fresh fish and protein bar with minimal time in the middle aisles where most of the processed foods are located.

You won't have to spend too much time on reading food labels if you are eating colorful, healthy, fresh and non-man-made foods. However, the food labels of such foods like quinoa, beans, pasta, rice, pumpkin, and cheese can assure you of the proper serving size, along with the macronutrient and micronutrient contents and, of course, the ingredients of that product.

The Q2 rule of thumb for ingredients of any product is the fewer the ingredients, the better. The order of the ingredients is also a way to evaluate the contents of that product starting with the first ingredient being the highest percentage content of the product and so on. Also, know what the ingredients are - if you do not then think again about that product. There are an abundant amount of chemicals and sugar additives on the market today and any one of them could end up on your plate. Yikes! Stay away from HFCS (high-fructose corn syrup), hydrogenated oil, chemicals and man-made food additives. Simply, know your ingredients and choose the foods with the least amount of ingredients. This component outweighs the well-known obsession of our society with carbohydrates and fat. Would you rather eat a high healthy fat or complex carbohydrate food with minimal ingredients or a lesser healthy fat and complex carbohydrate food with maximal ingredients? Think about that for a moment. Society and marketers have made our food product decisions confusing when it doesn't need to be.

If you eat animal or fish, then that could be just as confusing with words on the package like all-natural. Look for the Certified Organic label and Certified Non-GMO label along with words like grass-fed, wild caught – not farm raised or all-natural. Visiting your local butcher or organic farmer can also take the guess work out of what you are eating. The following grocery store list will support the Q2 recipes in this book, a staple in my kitchen and pantry - and hopefully now in yours.

VEGETABLES, Fresh
Asparagus
Broccoli
Brussels Sprouts
Cabbage, Purple
Cabbage, White
Carrot
Cauliflower
Celery
Cucumber
Cucumber, seedless
Eggplant
Garlic, clove
Green Beans
Mushrooms, Bella
Mushroom, Portabella
Mushroom, Shiitake
Mushroom, White
Onion, Green
Onion, Red
Onion, White
Onion, Yellow
Parsnip
Peapods
Peas, Snow
Peas, Sugar Snap
Pepper, Tri-Colored
Pepper, Green Bell
Pepper, Red Bell
Pepper, Serrano
Potatoes, White
Scallion
Shallot
Squash, Butternut

Squash, Kabocha
Squash, Spaghetti
Sweet Potato
Tomatillos
Tomatoes, Campari
Tomatoes, Heirloom
Tomatoes, Plum
Turnip
Zucchini

VEGGIES, Frozen
Edamame, shelled
Peas, Baby

FRESH SPICES
Basil
Chives
Cilantro
Dill
Ginger Root
Mint
Parsley
Thyme

OTHER
Artichokes, canned
Beets, pre-cooked
Figs, dried
Pumpkin, canned
Tomato, crushed-can
Tomato, sun-dried
Capers
Pickles, Sweet
Avocado Mayonnaise

Dijon Mustard
Hot Sauce
Liquid Aminos (Soy sauce alternative)
Worcestershire Sauce
Parchment Paper

LETTUCE
Collard Greens
Kale
Lettuce, wraps
Lettuce, Arugula
Lettuce, Boston
Lettuce, Butter
Lettuce, Mixed Green
Lettuce, Spring Mix
Spinach
Spinach, Baby
Swiss Chard
Kale, Spinach, Chard

FRUITS, Fresh
Apple, Golden
Apple, Granny Smith
Apple, red
Avocado
Banana
Blackberries
Blueberries
Cranberries
Grapes, green
Grapes, red
Kiwi
Lemon

Lime
Mango
Orange
Peach
Pear
Pineapple
Pomegranate
Raspberries
Strawberries

FRUIT, Frozen
Cherries
Mixed Berries
Strawberries

DRINKS
Coconut Water
Green Tea, caffeine
Green Tea, decaf
Kombucha, raw

DRIED SPICES
Basil
Bay Leaf
Black Pepper, Coarse
BlackPepper, Ground
Cayenne Pepper
Celery Salt
Cinnamon, Ground
Cloves, Ground
Coriander, ground
Cumin
Curry Powder
Garlic Powder

Ginger
Nutmeg
Onion Powder
Oregano
Paprika
Paprika, Smoked
Red Pepper Flakes
Salt, Kosher
Sea Salt, Fine-Grain
Thyme
Turmeric

BEANS
Multi, dried
Lentil
Miso
Tofu
BEANS, Canned
Black
Cannellini
Garbanzo
Red Kidney, light

SEEDS
Chia
Flaxseed, golden
Flaxseed Meal
Pumpkin
Sunflower
Sesame
Tahini

NUTS
Almonds, Raw

Almonds, Sliced
Almonds, Slivered
Pecans
Walnuts

GRAINS
Barley
Bread, 12-Grain
Wraps, Multi-Grain
Oats, Old-Fashioned
Oats, Steel-Cut
Polenta, Instant
Quinoa
Tempeh
Bread Crumbs, plain
Panko, gluten-free
Plant Protein Powder

RICE
Arborio
Black
Brown
Jasmine

STOCK
Beef, unsalted
Chicken, unsalted
Vegetable, unsalted

OIL
Avocado Oil
Ghee
Grapeseed Oil
Olive Oil

Olive Oil, Extra-virgin
Sesame Oil, toasted

VINEGAR
Apple Cider
Balsamic
Balsamic, White
Rice, seasoned
Sherry Wine
White Wine, dry

PASTA/ NOODLES
Chickpea
Quinoa
Rice

DAIRY/EGGS
Butter
Eggs
Greek Yogurt, plain
Greek Yogurt, vanilla
Heavy Cream
Milk, Almond
Milk, Coconut - raw
Milk, Soy

CHEESE
Blue Cheese
Cottage Cheese
Feta Cheese
Goat Cheese
Mozzarella
Parmesan, fresh
Ricotta Cheese

FISH
Cod
Crab, lump
Halibut
Salmon
Scallops
Sea Bass
Shrimp

ANIMAL
Chicken Breast
(skinless, boneless)
Pork Chop, center cut
Pork Tenderloin
Chuck Roast
Flank Steak

BAKING
Baking Powder
Baking Soda
Cocoa Powder,
Unsweetened
Extract, Almond
Extract, Pure Vanilla
Flour, Almond
Flour, Brown Rice

SWEET
Agave Nectar
Honey, Pure
Maple Syrup, Pure
Sugar, Almond
Sugar, Coconut

Q2 Fruit Tip: Cut your aging bananas into slices and put in a freezer-safe container to use at your convenience for smoothies, twice as nice cream or other delectable creations. Bought an overabundance of berries? Store them in the freezer until ready to use.

Re-Stock Your Kitchen

Your kitchen is probably already stocked with the gadgets, cookware, bakeware and utensils that you will need to create the Q2 recipes, along with your own healthy cooking creations. However, there are a few that I highly recommend that you have; a high-performance blender, an immersion blender and a food processor. These machines will complement your cooking skills, save you time and aid simplicity of healthy meals, snacks and smoothies. Also, keep readily available mason jars on hand so that you can create, store and transport, versus plastic containers. Re-evaluate your cookware and see if it is outdated. If it is, and if your pocketbook allows you to upgrade to a healthier version, then do so; it will be more beneficial to your health and the health of your family.

Let's talk oil a moment. It can be very confusing as to which ones to use. They are not all created equal, and it is in your best interest and health to stock your kitchen with various oils as they all have unique attributes and usage. The Q2 rule of thumb is, cook various foods at various temperatures with the right oil for optimal health benefits. The following guide will assist you and assure you:

- If you are cooking at super high temperatures, like frying or broiling, then use ghee (clarified butter) or avocado oil. Side note: Hopefully you are not frying.
- Up to 450 degrees, use avocado, ghee or soybean oil.

- Up to 400 degrees, use avocado, olive or grapeseed oil.
- Up to 350 degrees, use olive, grapeseed or coconut oil.
- Coconut oil is great for baking and sautéing.
- EVVO (Extra Virgin Olive Oil) can be used up to 350 degrees and sesame oil can be used up to 300 degrees, however, both EVVO and Sesame are best used as a dressing.

Start switching out some of your products that you may have used in the past for healthier ones, like liquid aminos in place of soy sauce, and even your lower-sodium soy sauce. Change up your meat choices with foods like beans, cauliflower and tempeh. Re-stock your kitchen and pantry with the ingredients that you will need to prep for the week, and let's do this!

Prep Week Made Simple

Map out your meals for the week. Write your grocery list. Go to the grocery store. This is half of the battle. Now the food is in your kitchen, ready to be used, transformed and ingested. I like to choose my meals for the week first then assign the days accordingly.

Here is a Q2 prep week example which always includes two smoothies, two breakfast meals, two dips, two salads, two vegetarian meals and at least two transformation meals.

The Green Goddess Smoothie (M, Tu, W)

Berry Blossom Smoothie (Th, F, Sa)

Beet Kale Muffins → Beet Burgers

Quick and Easy Egg Stacks

Slow Cooked Apple Pie Oats

Avocado Hummus → Green Creamy Quinoa Pasta w/Roasted Tomatoes

Artichoke Spinach Dip → Cod Fish Rolls

Kale Quinoa Salad

Chicory Salad w/Apple Cider Dressing

Tempeh Stir Fry

Miso Glazed Chicken → Miso Chicken Lettuce Wraps (can use cauliflower in place of chicken)

Healthy Shepherd's Pie Casserole (made with cauliflower, chicken, turkey, pork or beef)

Okay, I know what you are thinking – this doesn't look simple, but let me break it down for you even further. After all, if you fail to plan, then you will plan to fail. Keep in mind that the following meals and snacks are all ONE SERVING size - Quantity matters!

	Monday	Tuesday	Wednesday
Breakfast	Green Goddess Smoothie	Apple Pie Oats	Green Goddess Smoothie
Snack	Egg Stack	Beet Kale Muffin	Egg Stack
Lunch	Kale Quinoa Salad	Cod Fish Roll	Chicory Salad
Snack	Avocado Hummus w/ Carrot/Celery	Green Goddess Smoothie	Beet Kale Muffin
Dinner	Cod Fish Roll, Steamed Vegetable	Miso Glazed Chicken w/Quinoa/Veggies	Creamy Avocado Quinoa Pasta
Snack	1 T. Walnuts or Almonds	1 t. Almond Butter	1 T. Heart Healthy Granola

	Thursday	Friday	Saturday
Breakfast	Apple Pie Oats	Berry Blossom Smoothie	Apple Pie Oats
Snack	Berry Blossom Smoothie	Egg Stack	Berry Blossom Smoothie
Lunch	Miso Chicken Lettuce Wraps	Kale Quinoa Salad	Tempeh Stir Fry
Snack	Artichoke Spinach Dip Carrots/Celery	Beet Kale Muffin	1 T. Seeds (Pumpkin, Sunflower, other)
Dinner	Tempeh Stir Fry Black Rice	Healthy Sheppard's Pie	Beet Burger Chicory Salad
Snack	1 T. Seeds (Pumpkin, Sunflower, other)	1 t. Almond Butter	

We will just say that Sunday is your prep day, and if it is not, then you will simply change up your days to your schedule. Make your prep day super simple so that you have the time to plan and create. Sunday, Easy Plain Greek Yogurt Parfait: Layer Greek yogurt, fresh fruit and granola, eat leftovers or a serving of next week's creation, steamed veggies, fresh fruit, beans and rice or make the fast to-go-to chicken or fish parcels.

In this particular meal plan week, prep accordingly per day:

Sunday: Make Beet Kale Muffins, Easy Egg Stacks, Slow Cook Apple Pie Oats, Avocado Hummus, Artichoke Spinach Dip and Kale Quinoa Salad with extra quinoa and black rice for the week. Wash and cut up fruits and veggies for easy snacks and access. (Estimated prep time:

60-90 minutes, but keep in mind you will have minimal prep time for the remainder of the week)

Monday: Make three-day smoothie, cod fish rolls and steamed veggies and marinate the miso glazed chicken for Tuesday's dinner.

Tuesday: Make miso glazed chicken and veggies for dinner.

Wednesday: Make chicory salad and creamy avocado quinoa pasta.

Thursday: Make three-day smoothie and make tempeh stir fry for dinner.

Friday: Make healthy Shepherd's pie for dinner.

Saturday: Make beet burger and chicory salad.

Now can you see the simplicity? Even if you made half of these meals and had fresh fruit and veggies on hand, along with beans and lean proteins, you will be on the right track of fueling your body with all of the macronutrients that your body needs. Don't let this overwhelm you. Maybe you boil eggs and make quick and easy on-the-go snacks like nuts and seeds, carrot/celery sticks with homemade bean dip for the week. Take baby steps and cook what you are comfortable with. Enjoy! In turn, your body and mind will thank you!

Keep in mind that all of the Q2 Recipes have a proper ratio of macronutrients; healthy protein, healthy carbohydrates and healthy fats.

<u>Q2 Recipe Equivalent Measures</u>

1 dash = 2 to 3 drops

1 t. = 1 teaspoon

1 T. = 1 Tablespoon

¼ cup = 4 Tablespoons

1/3 cup = 5 Tablespoons + 1 teaspoon

½ cup = 8 Tablespoons

1 cup = 8 ounces

1 pound = 16 ounces

Chapter 9

Q2 Recipes

The easiest and most convenient way to eat colorful, green and plant based is to make a green drink or smoothie. By using a plant-based protein powder, you will enhance the nutrients of the fruits and vegetables, balance out the carbohydrates and natural sugars and allow your body to enjoy a healthy balance of the macronutrients, protein, carbs and fats that your body, mind and cells crave.

A full recipe makes approximately 60 ounces – that is six 10-ounce servings, and can fuel your whole family or can easily be stored in the refrigerator for up to three days for convenience. I prepare one recipe to last three days for two people a few times a week. Want to make less? Simply cut the recipe in half. Enjoy the variety of Q2 recipes that are as easy as 1, 2, 3!

GREEN DRINKS/SMOOTHIES

The Lean Green Machine (p. 118)
and Lean Green Machine Muffins (p. 148)

THE LEAN GREEN MACHINE

- 1 fresh lime, juiced
- 2 Granny Smith apples (preferably organic), unpeeled & cut into big pieces
- 1 orange, peeled
- 10 oz. spinach (about 8 cups)
- 1 banana, peeled
- 2 t. fresh ginger
- 2 cups ice

Q2 Recommendation: Add Plant Protein Powder* per package

1. Put juice of lime into a high-performance blender, add the apples and orange and blend.
2. Add half of the spinach, blend. Add ice and the remainder of the spinach, blend well.
3. Add protein powder, banana, ginger and blend until smooth.

Optional: Add water for desired consistency!

Serves 6.

Q2: 86 calories per serving, protein 2.5g, carbohydrates 21g, fat 0.5g, fiber 4.5g

For additional protein ~ add plant protein powder.

TRIPLE P (PEAR, PINEAPPLE & POWER GREENS)

- 2 pears, unpeeled & cut into big pieces
- 3 cups fresh pineapple, approximately ¾ of a fresh pineapple
- 10 oz. Power Green Mixture; Swiss chard, kale, spinach (about 8 cups)
- 1 banana
- 2 cups ice

Q2 Recommendation: Add Plant Protein Powder* per package

1. Place the pears and pineapple into a high-performance blender and blend.
2. Add half of the power green mixture, blend. Add ice and the remainder of the greens – blend well.
3. Add banana and protein powder and blend until smooth.

Optional: Add water for desired consistency!

Serves 6.

Q2: 125 calories per serving, protein 3.2g, carbohydrates 31g, fat 0.5g, fiber 5.4g

For additional protein ~ add plant protein powder.

THE GREEN GODDESS

- 1 fresh lime, juiced
- 2 mangos, peeled and sliced
- 2 cups fresh pineapple, approximately ½ of a fresh pineapple
- 5 oz. spinach (about 4 cups)
- 5 oz. kale (about 4 cups)
- 1 banana, peeled
- 2 cups ice

Q2 Recommendation: Add Plant Protein Powder* per package

1. Put juice of lime into a high-performance blender, add mangos and pineapple and blend.
2. Add the spinach, blend. Add ice and kale, blend well.
3. Add banana and protein powder and blend until smooth.

Optional: Add water for desired consistency!

Serves 6.

Q2: 132 calories per serving, protein 2.9g, carbohydrates 33g, fat 0.7g, fiber 4.3g

For additional protein ~ add plant protein powder.

BERRY BLOSSOM

- 2 cups strawberries, raspberries or blueberries or mixed berries
- 1 orange, peeled
- 1 apple (preferably organic), cut into big pieces
- 10 oz. Power Green Mixture, swiss chard, kale, spinach (about 8 cups)
- 1 banana, peeled
- 3 T. chia seeds
- 2 cups ice

Q2 Recommendation: Add Plant Protein Powder* per package

1. Place the berries, orange and apple into a high-performance blender and blend.
2. Add half of the power green mixture, blend. Add ice and the remainder of the greens, blend well.
3. Add banana, chia seeds and protein powder and blend until smooth.

Optional: Add water for desired consistency!

Serves 6.

Q2: 107 calories per serving, protein 3.3g, carbohydrates 25.4g, fat 0.6g, fiber 5g

For additional protein ~ add plant protein powder.

MANGO-BERRY

- 2 mangos, peeled and sliced
- 2 cups strawberries
- 1 orange, peeled
- 10 oz. Power Greens; Swiss chard, spinach and kale (about 8 cups)
- 1 banana
- 2 cups ice

Q2 Recommendation: Add Plant Protein Powder* per package

1. Place the mango, berries and orange into a high-performance blender and blend.
2. Add half of the power green mixture, blend. Add ice and the remainder of the greens, blend well.
3. Add banana and protein powder and blend until smooth.

Optional: Add water for desired consistency!

Serves 6.

Q2: 141 calories per serving, protein 4g, carbohydrates 33.6g, fat 0.9g, fiber 5.5g

For additional protein ~ add plant protein powder.

GREENDRINK.COM (CRANBERRY, ORANGE, MANGO)

- 1 cup of fresh cranberries (whole and cleaned)
- 2 oranges
- 2 mangos, peeled and sliced
- 10 oz. spinach (about 8 cups)
- 1 banana
- 2 cups ice

Q2 Recommendation: Add Plant Protein Powder* per package

1. Put cranberries, oranges and mangos into a high-performance blender and blend.
2. Add half of the spinach, blend. Add ice and the remainder of the spinach, blend well.
3. Add banana and protein powder and blend until smooth.

Optional: Add water for desired consistency!

Serves 6.

Q2: 134 calories per serving, protein 3.1g, carbohydrates 31.9g, fat 0.7g, fiber 5.5g

For additional protein ~ add plant protein powder.

POT OF GOLD

- 5 oz. kale (approximately 4 cups)
- 2 golden apples, unpeeled & cut into big pieces
- 3 cups fresh pineapple, approximately ¾ of a fresh pineapple
- 1 cup of green grapes
- 1 banana
- 1 T. ground Flaxseed
- 2 cups ice

Q2 Recommendation: Add Plant Protein Powder* per package

1. Put apples, pineapple and grapes into a high-performance blender and blend.
2. Add half of the kale, blend. Add ice and the remainder of the kale, blend well.
3. Add banana, flaxseed meal and protein powder and blend until smooth.

Optional: Add water for desired consistency!

Serves 6.

Q2: 125 calories per serving, protein 1.9g, carbohydrates 31g, fat 0.7g, fiber 4.3g

*For additional protein ~ add plant protein powder.

CHERRY CHIA COCONUT

- 1 10-ounce bag pitted frozen cherries
- 2 cups pineapple, approximately ½ of a fresh pineapple
- 1 frozen banana
- 10 oz. spinach (about 8 cups)
- 12 oz. coconut water, 100% raw unsweetened
- 2 T. chia seeds
- 2 cups ice

Q2 Recommendation: Add Plant Protein Powder* per package

1. Put cherries, pineapple and frozen bananas into a high-performance blender and blend.
2. Add half of the spinach, blend. Add ice and the remainder of the spinach, blend well.
3. Add unsweetened coconut milk, chia seeds and protein powder and blend until smooth.

Optional: Add water for desired consistency!

Serves 6.

Q2: 185 calories per serving, protein 4.1g, carbohydrates 40.3g, fat 2.7g, fiber 7g

For additional protein ~ add plant protein powder.

KIWI SURPRISE

- 6 kiwi, peeled and halved
- 1 apple, unpeeled and cut into big pieces
- 1 cup vanilla greek yogurt, 0%
- 1 frozen banana
- 5 oz. spinach (about 4 cups)
- 1 T. ground flax seed
- 2 cups ice

Q2 Recommendation: Add Plant Protein Powder* per package

1. Put kiwi, apple, yogurt and banana into a high-performance blender and blend.
2. Add the spinach, blend well.
3. Add ground flaxseed and protein powder and blend until smooth.

Optional: Add water for desired consistency!

Serves 6.

Q2: 118 calories per serving, protein 4.6g, carbohydrates 25.3g, fat 1g, fiber 4.5g

For additional protein ~ add plant protein powder.

BANANA SPLIT

- 1 cup fresh or frozen strawberries
- 2 cups fresh pineapple, approximately ½ of the pineapple
- 1 frozen banana
- 1 ½ cups coconut milk, 100% - unsweetened
- 5 oz. spinach (about 4 cups)
- 1 T. ground flaxseed
- 2 cups ice

Q2 Recommendation: Add Plant Protein Powder* per package

1. Put strawberries, pineapple and banana into a high-performance blender and blend.
2. Add the spinach and coconut milk, blend well.
3. Add flaxseed and protein powder and blend until smooth.

Optional: Add water for desired consistency!

Serves 6.

Q2: 135 calories per serving, protein 3.2g, carbohydrates 16.9g, fat 6.6g, fiber 2.6g

For additional protein ~ add plant protein powder.

AVOCADO DELIGHT

- 2 avocados, peeled and halved
- 2 cups fresh pineapple, approximately ½ of the pineapple
- 1 frozen banana
- 1 cup almond, soy or raw coconut milk - unsweetened
- 5 oz. spinach (about 4 cups)
- 1 T. ground flax seed
- 2 cups ice

Q2 Recommendation: Add Plant Protein Powder* per package

1. Put avocado, pineapple and banana into a high-performance blender and blend.
2. Add the spinach and milk, blend well.
3. Add ground flaxseed and protein powder and blend until smooth.

Optional: Add water for desired consistency!

Serves 6.

Q2: 199 calories per serving, protein 3.7g, carbohydrates 19.1g, fat 13.5g, fiber 6g

For additional protein ~ add plant protein powder.

GREEN SHAKE SALAD

- 3 medium-sized campari or vine tomatoes
- 2 celery stalks, cut into big pieces
- ½ large seedless cucumber or 1 regular cucumber
- 1 avocado
- 1 T. fresh parsley
- 5 oz. Swiss Chard (about 4 cups)
- 2 cups ice

Q2 Recommendation: Add Plant Protein Powder* per package

1. Put tomatoes, celery, cucumber, avocado and parsley into a high-performance blender and blend.
2. Add the spinach and ice, blend well.
3. Add protein powder and blend until smooth.

Optional: Add water for desired consistency!

Serves 6.

Q2: 70 calories per serving, protein 2g, carbohydrates 6.9g, fat 4.7g, fiber 3.5g

*For additional protein ~ add plant protein powder

THE EMERALD FOREST

- ½ fresh lime, juiced
- ½ fresh lemon, juiced
- 1 orange, peeled
- 2 apples, unpeeled and cut into big pieces
- 1 cup pineapple, approximately ¼ of a fresh pineapple
- ½ large seedless cucumber
- 1 celery stalk, cut into big pieces
- 1 large carrot, scrubbed with skin, cut into big pieces
- ¼ cup fresh flat parsley
- Couple of sprigs of fresh mint
- 5 oz. Swiss Chard (about 4 cups)
- 2 cups of ice

Q2 Recommendation: Add Plant Protein Powder* per package

1. Put the juice of a lime and lemon, orange, apples and pineapple into a high-performance blender and blend.
2. Add the cucumber, celery, carrot, parsley and mint and blend. Add ice and spinach, blend well.
3. Add protein powder and blend until smooth.

Optional: Add water for desired consistency!

Serves 6.

Q2: 82 calories per serving, protein 1.6g, carbohydrates 20.8g, fat 0.3g, fiber 4.2g

For additional protein ~ add plant protein powder.

GREEN TEA SMOOTHIE

- 2 cups green grapes
- 1 frozen banana
- 2 cups green tea, brewed (caffeinated or decaf)
- 5 oz. spinach (about 4 cups)
- 2 cups ice

Q2 Recommendation: Add Plant Protein Powder* per package

1. Put grapes and banana into a high-performance blender and blend.
2. Add the spinach and green tea, blend well.
3. Add protein powder and blend until smooth.

Optional: Add water for desired consistency!

Serves 4.

Q2: 65 calories per serving, protein 1.6g, carbohydrates 15.9g, fat 0.4g, fiber 2g

For additional protein ~ add plant protein powder.

DRINKS

Watermelon Mint Drink (p. 134)
Festive Kale Salad (p. 179)
Harvest Polenta Pizza (p. 203)
Eggplant Parmigiana Polenta Pizza (p. 201)

EVERYONE HAS A go-to drink when they want a little flavor. Kombucha is a great choice, and if you are unfamiliar with it, it is a fermented tea that contains electrolytes, polyphenols, enzymes and probiotics, and it comes in various flavors. Check it out at your local grocery in the cold drink section, but make sure that you reach for the organic and raw kombucha.

Transform your favorite hot tea. Steep the tea, let it cool then put it over ice. Add a variety of flavors to your liking; honey, lemon, ginger, herbs or other flavorful choices.

Pulsed watermelon with fresh mint is also a great choice, a delightful way to hydrate and energize. Watermelon naturally balances out your digestive system and flushes out your kidneys. Watermelon contains over 90% water and the health benefits are endless.

Your water intake does not have to be boring. Just add color and flavor to your water, try a recipe or create your own flavors.

Mint Water – add a sprig of fresh mint

Basil Water – add fresh basil

Turmeric Water – add fresh turmeric root or ground turmeric

Cucumber Water – add cucumber slices

Lemon and/or Lime Water – add lemon slices and/or lime slices

Citrus Water – add orange, lemons and lime slices

Berry Water – add fresh berries

Kiwi Strawberry Water – add peeled and sliced kiwi and strawberry

Lemon, Cucumber, Mint Water – add lemon slices, cucumber and mint

Lime, Cucumber, Ginger Root, Mint Water – add lime, cucumber, ginger root and mint

The combinations are endless!

BREAKFAST, SNACK or ANY TIME

Breakfast is the most important meal of the day. Strive to eat within one hour of waking to boost your metabolism, fuel your brain and prepare to seize the day. The following recipes also make great snacks or anytime meals. Simply start your day with a smoothie if you choose or prepare these delicious and nutritious meals to start your day.

Festive Oatmeal

1. Place fresh raspberries at the bottom of the bowl.

2. Saute diced peaches with a pinch of salt (for slight sweet and saltiness) while you cook ½ cup steel-cut oats.

3. Top the raspberries with cooked steel-cut oats, a little pure honey and top it with sautéed peaches, slivered almonds, pumpkins seeds and chia seeds.

Slow Cooked Apple Pie Oats - Page 137   Egg Omelet Muffins - Page 144

Spinach Artichoke Mushroom
Frittata - Page 146

Beet Kale Muffins - Page 147

SLOW COOKED APPLE PIE OATS

- 2 medium apples – 1 red, 1 green – cored and diced with skin left on
- 1 cup steel-cut oats
- 2 cups almond milk or coconut milk, unsweetened
- 1 T. pure maple syrup
- 1 T. pure honey
- ½ lemon, juiced
- 2 T. flax seed meal
- 1 ½ t. ground cinnamon
- ¾ t. ground nutmeg
- ¼ t. fine-grain sea salt

Q2 Option: Garnish with slivered raw almonds and/or pumpkin seeds

1. Grease a slow cooker with coconut oil.
2. Combine all ingredients in the slow cooker – blend well.
3. Cook on high for 3 hours then switch to low for 1 hour or cook on low for 8 hours.

Scoop ½ cup in bowl for a healthy breakfast, snack or condiment.

Serves 4.

Q2: 173 calories per serving, protein: 2.6g, carbohydrates: 32.7g, fat: 4.1g, fiber 5.7g

OVERNIGHT COLD BANANA PIE OATS

- 1 banana, smashed
- 1/3 cup old-fashioned rolled oats
- ½ cup almond milk, unsweetened
- ¼ cup plain Greek yogurt, 0%
- 1 T. pure honey
- ½ t. p vanilla extract
- 1 t. flax seed meal

Q2 Option: Garnish with unsalted almonds or salted for slightly sweet and salty.

1. Combine all ingredients in a bowl, blend well.
2. Cover and refrigerate overnight or for at least 8 hours.
3. Enjoy!

Q2 Tip: Store in an easy to-go container like a mason jar.

One Serving.

Q2: 278 calories per serving, protein: 8.5g, carbohydrates: 56.1g, fat: 3.5g, fiber 5.5g

OVERNIGHT COLD MAPLE PECAN OATS

- 1/3 cup old-fashioned rolled oats
- ½ cup almond milk, unsweetened
- ¼ cup plain Greek yogurt, 0%
- 2 t. pure maple syrup
- ¼ t. pure vanilla extract
- 1t. ground cinnamon
- 1 t. chia seeds
- 1 T. pecans, unsalted or salted for slightly sweet and salty

1. Combine all ingredients in a bowl, blend well.
2. Cover and refrigerate overnight or for at least 8 hours.
3. Enjoy!

Q2 Tip: Store in an easy to-go container like a mason jar.

One Serving.

Q2: 374 calories per serving, protein: 13g, carbohydrates: 36.1g, fat: 21.1g, fiber 14.3g

HEART HEALTHY GRANOLA

- 3 cups old-fashioned rolled oats
- 1 cup shredded coconut, unsweetened
- ¾ cup raw pumpkin seeds, unsalted
- ¾ cup raw sunflower seeds, unsalted
- ¾ cup slivered almonds, unsalted
- ¾ cup walnuts, chopped
- ½ cup ground flax seed meal
- ¼ cup golden flax seeds
- ¼ cup chia seeds
- ½ cup pure maple syrup
- ½ cup coconut oil
- 1 t. ground cinnamon
- ½ t. ground nutmeg
- ½ t. fine sea salt

Q2 Recommendation: 2 T. Plant Protein Powder*

1. Combine all the ingredients in a large bowl, blend well.
2. Lightly grease two large baking sheets with coconut oil.
3. Spread the mixture in a single layer for each baking sheet.

Bake: 325 degrees for 15 minutes, then stir gently and continue baking for an additional 15 minutes. Let cool completely.

Serves 24.

Q2: 206 calories per serving, protein: 5.7g, carbohydrates: 15.5g, fat: 14.5g, fiber 3.8g

For additional protein ~ add plant protein powder.

SLOW COOKED APPLE QUINOA PORRIDGE

- 2 medium apples – 1 red, 1 green – cored and diced with skin left on
- 1 cup uncooked quinoa
- 2 cups almond milk or coconut milk, unsweetened
- 1 T. pure maple syrup
- 1 T. pure honey
- 1 t. pure vanilla extract
- 2 T. flax seed meal
- 1 T. chia seeds
- 2 t. ground cinnamon
- 1 t. ground nutmeg

Q2 Option: Garnish with slivered raw almonds and/or pumpkin seeds

1. Grease a slow cooker with coconut oil.
2. Combine all ingredients in the slow cooker – blend well.
3. Cook on a low setting for 6 hours.

Scoop 1/3 cup in bowl for a healthy breakfast, snack or condiment.

Serves 8.

Q2: 164 calories per serving, protein: 4.1g, carbohydrates: 28.1g, fat: 4.1g, fiber 5.2g

SLOW COOKED PUMPKIN QUINOA PORRIDGE

- 15 oz. can pumpkin
- 1 cup uncooked quinoa
- 2 cups almond milk or coconut milk, unsweetened
- 4 T. pure honey
- 1 t. pure vanilla extract
- 2 T. flax seed meal
- 1 T. chia seeds
- 1 t. ground cinnamon
- 1 t. ground nutmeg
- ½ t. ground cloves

Q2 Option: Garnish with slivered raw almonds and/or pumpkin seeds

1. Grease a slow cooker with coconut oil.
2. Combine all ingredients in the slow cooker, blend well.
3. Cook on a low setting for 6 hours.

Scoop 1/3 cup in bowl for a healthy breakfast, snack or condiment.

Serves 8.

Q2: 256 calories per serving, protein: 4.4g, carbohydrates: 25.5g, fat: 16.9g, fiber 5.6g

EGG AVOCADO PEPPER BOAT

- 1 large red pepper, cut length-wise in half and seeded
- 1 avocado, cut length-wise in half and pitted
- 1 egg

1. Place the red pepper halves in a baking dish open side up.
2. Scoop out each of the halved avocado from the skin and place in the peppers.
3. Whisk the egg and pour into the hole of the avocado.

Bake: 350 degrees for 20 minutes or until toothpick comes out clean.

Great for a meal or a healthy snack.

Serves 2.

Q2: 195 calories per serving, protein: 5.1g, carbohydrates: 12.1g, fat: 15.7g, fiber 6.7g

Egg Avocado Pepper Boat

EGG OMELET MUFFINS

▷ 2 cups of vegetables to your liking (for example, asparagus, mushrooms, bell peppers, spinach)

▷ ½ cup asparagus, washed, trimmed and cut in small chunks (use the upper half of the stalk)

▷ ½ cup mushrooms, washed, trimmed and cut in small chunks

▷ ½ cup bell peppers, washed, trimmed and cut in small chunks

▷ ½ cup baby spinach, washed, trimmed and cut in small pieces

▷ 12 organic non-GMO Eggs

1. Preheat oven to 375 degrees. Grease muffin pan with avocado oil.

2. Combine veggies in a bowl then fill each muffin ¾ high.

3. Whisk eggs thoroughly and fill each muffin tin to the top.

Bake: 375 degrees for 15-20 minutes, until slightly brown and toothpick comes out clean. Immediately loosen the edges with a thin spatula for easy removal.

Makes 12 muffins.

Q2: 74 calories per egg muffin, protein: 6.3g, carbohydrates: 0.8g, fat: 5g, fiber 0.3g

QUICK AND EASY EGG STACK

Crust:

- 1 cup instant polenta
- 3 cups water
- 1 t. fine-grain sea salt

Eggs:

- 6 whole eggs + 6 egg whites, organic non-GMO

Topping:

- Various vegetables, spinach, mushrooms, artichokes, peppers, asparagus, etc.
- feta cheese or other cheese of your choice (optional)
- Dash fine-grain sea salt
- Dash black pepper

1. Cook polenta per package directions. Spoon and press the creamy cooked polenta into individual ramekins of desired size.
2. Sauté the vegetables in a lightly greased pan until lightly softened. Add a dash of salt and pepper. Transfer the vegetables to a bowl.
3. In a separate bowl, whisk the eggs then cook in the same lightly greased pan with a dash of salt and pepper. Place a scoop of eggs in the ramekin on the polenta and stack the remaining ramekin with vegetables and top with cheese, if you would like.

Enjoy! Or place in refrigerator for the week to reheat for a readily available egg breakfast or healthy snack.

Makes 4 ramekins.

Q2: 155 calories per ramekin/serving, protein: 14.7g, carbohydrates: 8.5g, fat: 6.7g, fiber 0.6g

SPINACH, ARTICHOKE, MUSHROOM AND RED PEPPER FRITTATA

) 12 organic non-GMO Eggs

) 1 cup baby spinach, washed, trimmed and cut in small pieces

) 1 cup artichoke hearts, diced in small chunks

) 1 cup mushrooms, washed, trimmed and cut in small chunks

) 1 cup red bell pepper, washed, trimmed and cut in small chunks

) 1 small shallot, chopped

) 1 cup ricotta cheese

) ¼ cup feta cheese

) ½ t. fine-grain sea salt

) ½ t. ground black pepper

1. Combine spinach, artichoke, mushroom, red pepper and shallot in a bowl.

2. In a separate large bowl, whisk the eggs, then fold in the ricotta and feta cheese, salt and pepper, mix well.

3. Pour the veggies into the egg mixture, blend well, then pour into a greased 9-inch- deep pie plate or quiche pan.

Bake: 375 degrees for 40-45 minutes or until toothpick comes out clean.

Serves 6.

Q2: 229 calories per serving, protein: 18.5g, carbohydrates: 5.8g, fat: 14.7g, fiber 0.9g

BEET KALE MUFFINS

Base Recipe to use for the following Beet Muffins, Salad on page 173 and Beet Burgers on page 217:

- 1 cup kale, chopped finely
- 4 baby beets
- 1 cup cooked quinoa, which is about ½ cup of uncooked quinoa
- ¾ cup walnuts, chopped

- 1 cup almond flour or rice flour
- 1 t. baking soda
- 1 t. baking powder
- ½ t. fine-grain sea salt
- ¼ cup pure honey
- 1 t. pure vanilla extract

Q2 Recommendation: 2 T. Plant Protein Powder*

1. Combine the dry ingredients – flour, baking soda, baking powder, salt and plant protein.
2. Add the base kale mixture and honey, mix well.
3. Fill lined muffin holders to the top with the batter.

Bake: 350 degrees for 20-25 minutes or until toothpick comes out clean

Makes 12 muffins.

Q2: 174 calories per muffin/serving, protein: 3.5g, carbohydrates: 16.1g, fat: 10.1g, fiber 2.9g

For additional protein ~ add plant protein powder.

LEAN GREEN MACHINE MUFFINS

- 2 cups of The Lean Green Machine recipe – on page 118)
- 2 cups almond flour or rice flour
- 1 t. baking soda
- 1 t. baking powder
- 2 t. cinnamon
- ½ t. fine-grain sea salt
- 3/4 cup coconut oil
- 2 eggs
- 2 t. pure vanilla extract
- 1/2 cup pure honey

Q2 Recommendation: 2 T. Plant Protein Powder*

1. Combine the dry ingredients – Flour, baking soda, baking powder, cinnamon, salt and plant protein and set aside.
2. Blend the coconut oil and honey in a large bowl. Add egg one at a time, then add vanilla. Mix in half of the dry ingredients. Add 2 cups of the green machine recipe, blend well, then mix in the remaining dry ingredients.
3. Place batter ¾ full for each muffin in a lined muffin tin.

Bake: 350 degrees for 20-25 minutes or until toothpick comes out clean

Makes 20 muffins.

Q2: 124 calories per muffin/serving, protein*: 0.7g, carbohydrates: 12.1g, fat: 7g, fiber 1.8g

For additional protein ~ add plant protein powder.

DIPS, DRESSING & SAUCE

Goat Cheese Guacamole - Page 155

Quinoa Lemon Pepper
Hummus - Page 153

Roasted Red Pepper
Eggplant Dip - Page 157

The Making of Giardiniera
Hummus - Page 150

HOMEMADE HUMMUS

Base:

- 1 15-ounce can garbanzo beans (Chickpeas)
- ¼ cup organic tahini
- 4 T. water
- 2 T. extra-virgin olive oil

Q2 Tip: Make the base and then add whatever flavor you would like – see suggestions below.

1. Rinse the garbanzo beans thoroughly.
2. Blend the tahini and olive oil in a food processor until mixed well.
3. Add the garbanzo beans, water, and whatever flavor and blend until smooth.

Refrigerate for at least one hour before serving.

Serves 6.

Q2: 167 calories per base serving, protein: 5.6g, carbohydrates: 14g, fat: 11.2g, fiber 2.6g

Q2 Options: Omit the tahini and add additional olive oil for a creamier texture.

Add one of the following flavors or create your own favorite flavor:

- Garlic: Add 1 garlic clove
- Green Onion: Add 2 T. green onion
- Lemon: Add juice from one lemon and only put 2 T. Water
- Roasted Red Pepper: Roast a red pepper on grill top or in oven and add
- Spiced: With your favorite spices
- Spicy: Add 1-2 t. hot giardiniera

AVOCADO HUMMUS

- 1 15-ounce can cannellini beans, rinsed and drained
- 1 cup baby spinach
- 1 avocado, ripe
- 1 T. extra-virgin olive oil
- 1 fresh lemon, juiced
- 2 garlic cloves, minced
- Fine-grain sea salt, to taste
- Ground black pepper, to taste

Q2 Tip: Enjoy with raw vegetables or use it in a wrap or topping for pasta, chicken or fish.

One Step: Mix and smash all ingredients in a bowl by hand or hand mixer or put all ingredients in food processor. Can be served immediately.

Q2 Favorite: Use this as a dressing over Quinoa Pasta – see page 204

Serves 8.

Q2: 232 calories per serving, protein: 13.2g, carbohydrates: 34.9g, fat: 5.6g, fiber 15g

CREAMY EDAMAME HUMMUS

- 14 oz. shelled edamame, cooked per package instructions
- ¼ cup organic tahini
- 3 T. extra-virgin olive oil
- 4 T. water
- 1 fresh lemon, juiced
- 1 garlic clove
- ¾ t. cumin
- ¾ t. fine-grain sea salt

Q2 Tip: Enjoy with raw vegetables and healthier crackers or to compliment a meal.

1. Place the tahini and olive oil in a food processor until mixed well.
2. Add the edamame, water, lemon, garlic, cumin and salt – blend until smooth.

Refrigerate for at least one hour before serving.

Serves 6.

Q2: 208 calories per serving, protein: 8.9g, carbohydrates: 9.6g, fat: 16g, fiber 3.4

QUINOA LEMON PEPPER HUMMUS

- 1 cup quinoa, cooked – approximately ½ cup uncooked
- 1 can garbanzo beans (chickpeas)
- 3 T. extra-virgin olive oil
- 1 fresh lemon, juiced
- ¼ t. ground black pepper
- 1/8 t. fine-grain sea salt

Optional: Garnish with fresh parsley

Q2 Tip: Let the quinoa cool completely before preparing the recipe.

1. Rinse the garbanzo beans thoroughly.
2. Place all the ingredients in a food processor – blend until smooth.

Can be served immediately. Garnish with fresh parsley.

Serves 6.

Q2: 135 calories per serving, protein: 4.1g, carbohydrates: 17.4g, fat: 5.9g, fiber 1.3g

SALSA VERDE W/A KICK

- 1 lb. tomatillos, paper skins removed
- 3 serrano peppers, stems removed and chopped
- 2 garlic cloves, minced
- ½ cup fresh cilantro, chopped
- 1 T. kosher salt

Q2 Tip: For a milder salsa, seed and devein the peppers first.

1. Place tomatillos in a medium saucepan, cover with cold water, and bring to a simmer over medium heat. Cook until tomatillos are just soft but not falling apart, about 10 minutes.

2. Drain well.

3. Place tomatillo and remaining ingredients in a food processor and blend until almost smooth. Caution: Do not over blend or the salsa will be watery.

Refrigerate for at least one hour before serving.

Serves 8.

Q2: 20 calories per serving, protein: 0.7g, carbohydrates: 3.8g, fat: 0.6g, fiber 1.2

GOAT CHEESE GUACAMOLE

- 3 avocados, ripe – peeled, pitted and quartered
- 5 oz. goat cheese or ½ cup crumbled goat cheese
- ½ cup sun-dried tomatoes
- ¼ cup chives, fresh and chopped
- 1 T. olive oil
- 2 T. lemon juice, freshly squeezed
- 1/8 t. fine-grain sea salt
- 1/8 t. ground black pepper

Q2 Option: Make it spicy and add 1/8 t. cayenne pepper.

One Step: Blend all ingredients with an immersion blender or hand mixer. For best results, refrigerate for at least one hour before serving as a dip.

Q2 Recommendation: Serve with meals, as an appetizer or enjoy with raw vegetables.

Serves 8.

Q2: 174 calories per serving, protein: 4.7g, carbohydrates: 6.4g, fat: 15.5g, fiber 4.6g

PEACH GUACAMOLE (OR MANGO)

- 2 avocados, ripe, peeled, pitted and quartered
- 1 peach, ripe, peel on, pitted and diced
- 1 fresh lime, juiced
- 1 serrano pepper, seeded and thinly chopped
- 1 T. shallot, thinly chopped
- 1/8 t. fine-grain sea salt

Q2 Tip: For mango guacamole, substitute the peach for a peeled, seeded mango, also diced.

One Step: Blend and smash all ingredients by hand for a chunkier dip or blend with an immersion blender or hand mixer for a creamier dip. For best results, refrigerate for at least one hour before serving as a dip.

Q2 Recommendation: Serve with meals, as an appetizer or enjoy with raw vegetables.

Serves 6.

Q2: 111 calories per serving, protein: 1.5g, carbohydrates: 8.8g, fat: 9g, fiber 4.7g

ROASTED RED PEPPER EGGPLANT DIP

- 2 large red bell peppers, cut in half and cored
- 1 large eggplant, cut in half with peel
- 2 garlic cloves, peeled
- 2 T. plain Greek yogurt, 0%
- ½ t. paprika
- ½ t. coarsely-ground black pepper
- ¼ t. fine-grain sea salt

Optional: fresh basil, to garnish

1. Season the red pepper and eggplant with sea salt and pepper. Place the eggplant (peel side down), red pepper and garlic cloves on a parchment-lined baking pan. Bake at 400 degrees for 30-35 minutes or until slightly brown. Remove from oven and let cool.

Q2 Option: Sprinkle parmesan cheese on the eggplant the last 5 minutes of baking.

2. Scrape the first layer of the eggplant off and discard. Scoop out eggplant and put in a high-performance blender or food processor, blend until smooth.

3. Add the roasted pepper, garlic cloves, yogurt, paprika, black pepper and salt.

For best results, refrigerate for at least one hour before serving as a dip. Garnish with fresh basil.

Serves 6.

Q2: 60 calories per serving, protein: 6.2g, carbohydrates: 9.9g, fat: 0.3g, fiber 3.3g

SPINACH ARTICHOKE DIP

- 1 cup plain Greek yogurt, 0%
- 1 cup spinach, sautéed
- 1 cup artichoke hearts, chopped
- 1 T. bell pepper, chopped
- 1 T. carrot, chopped
- 1 T. onion, chopped
- ¼ cup parmesan cheese, fresh
- ½ t. fine-grain sea salt

Q2 Tip: Make ahead of time and chill in the refrigerator for at least one hour. Serve with raw veggies, use as a spread or in White Fish Rolls on page 226.

One Step: Mix all ingredients in a large bowl. For best results, refrigerate for at least one hour before serving as a dip.

Serves 6.

Q2: 59 calories per serving, protein: 5.5g, carbohydrates: 8.4g, fat: 1g, fiber 3.8g

TZATZIKI SAUCE

- 16 oz. plain Greek yogurt, 0%
- 1 cup cucumber, peeled and diced small
- 2 garlic cloves, peeled and minced
- 2 T. olive oil
- 1 T. fresh dill, chopped
- ½ fresh lemon, juiced
- Fine-grain sea salt, to taste
- Ground black pepper, to taste

Q2 Tip: Use to complement meals and appetizers or enjoy with raw vegetables.

One Step: Combine all ingredients thoroughly in a bowl. Taste for flavor and add salt and/or pepper, to your liking. Keep chilled until ready to use.

Q2 Favorite: Serve with Baked Edamame Falafel on page 215

Serves 8.

Q2: 69 calories per serving, protein: 6.1g, carbohydrates: 4.5g, fat: 3.6g, fiber 0.4g

LEMON DIPPING SAUCE

- 1 cup of plain Greek yogurt, 0%
- 1 T. lemon juice, freshly squeezed
- 1 t. Worcestershire sauce
- 1 t. parsley, fresh and chopped
- ½ t. garlic clove, minced
- Pinch of lemon zest

Q2 Tip: Use to complement meals and appetizers or enjoy with raw vegetables.

One Step: Combine all ingredients thoroughly in a bowl. Garnish with lemon zest. Keep chilled until ready to use.

Q2 Favorite: Pairs well with Brussels Sprout Chips Page 163 and Crab Balls on Page 167.

Serves 6.

Q2: 15 calories per serving, protein: 2.5g, carbohydrates: 1.3g, fat: 0g, fiber 0g

APPETIZERS & HEALTHY SNACKS

Cauliflower Buffalo Bites
- Page 165

Quinoa Crab Rolls - Page 167

ANGEL EGGS

- 12 eggs, hard boiled, cooled and peeled
- 15 oz. cannellini beans, rinsed and drained
- 4 T. plain Greek yogurt, 0%
- ¼ cup chopped celery
- 2 T. green onion, sliced
- ½ t. celery salt
- ¼ t. ground black pepper
- Paprika, to garnish and flavor

Q2 Tip: Use any remainder mixture as a dip – add additional chopped celery and green onion.

1. Cut eggs in half and remove the yolks. Place four whole egg yolks in a food processor and discard the rest. Place the egg whites open side up on a serving dish.

2. Add the beans, yogurt, celery, green onion, lemon, mustard, pepper and salt to the food processor. Blend until smooth and creamy.

3. Fill each egg half with the mixture and sprinkle with paprika.

Makes 24.

Q2: 92 calories per half egg, protein: 7.3g, carbohydrates: 11g, fat: 2.3g, fiber 4.5g

BRUSSELS SPROUT CHIPS –
SERVE WITH LEMON DIPPING SAUCE

- 1 lb. Brussels sprouts
- 1 T. grapeseed or olive oil
- Fine-grain sea salt or seasoned salt, to taste

Q2 Tip: Lightly grease a baking sheet with avocado oil. Wash the sprouts thoroughly with an apple cider vinegar bath. (See Page 102). If any layers of the sprouts come loose after washing, then sprinkle them around the baking dish with the intact sprouts.

1. Cut the thick stems of the Brussels sprouts and then cut lengthwise in half.

2. Wash and thoroughly squeeze out the excess water by using a salad spinner.

3. Place the sprouts cut-size up on the baking sheet. Drizzle the Brussels sprouts with olive oil and sprinkle with salt. (Remember, you can always add more salt – less is best)

Bake at 400 degrees for 15 minutes, then flip the sprouts over and cook for another 15 minutes or until brown and crispy. Serve with the Lemon Dipping Sauce on Page 160.

Serves 4.

Q2: 54 calories per serving, protein: 3.9g, carbohydrates: 10.5g, fat: 0.8g, fiber 4.4

KALE CHIPS

- 1 lb. kale, bunch - long stem
- 1 T. olive oil or flavored olive oil
- Fine-grain sea salt or seasoned salt, to taste

Q2 Tip: Line a non-insulated cookie sheet with parchment paper for best results. Wash the kale thoroughly with an apple cider vinegar bath. (See Page 102).

1. Remove the leaves from the thick stems of the kale and tear into bite size pieces.

2. Wash and thoroughly squeeze out the excess water by using a salad spinner.

3. Place the kale in a single layer on a baking sheet. Drizzle the kale with olive oil and sprinkle with salt. (Remember, you can always add more salt – less is best).

Bake at 325 degrees for 10-15 minutes or until the edges brown slightly.

Serves 4.

Q2: 86 calories per serving, protein: 3.4g, carbohydrates: 11.9g, fat: 3.5g, fiber 1.7

CAULIFLOWER BUFFALO BITES

- ½ cup rice flour
- ½ cup water
- 1 t. garlic powder
- ½ t. fine-grain sea salt
- 1 head cauliflower, cut into bite-size pieces
- 1 t. butter, melted
- 1 t. water
- ½ cup hot sauce of your choice
- Optional:
- ¼ bleu cheese, crumbled
- ¼ cup plain Greek yogurt, 0%

Q2 Tip: This is a great replacement for fat-infused chicken wings.

1. Combine in a large bowl; flour, water, garlic powder and salt and blend well.

2. Toss the cauliflower pieces in the batter and coat well. Place each piece on a baking sheet seasoned lightly with grapeseed oil. Bake the cauliflower for 8 minutes at 425 degrees, then flip to cook for an additional 8 minutes. Take out and cool for 5 minutes.

3. Combine melted butter, water and hot sauce in a large bowl and toss the baked cauliflower to coat well. Place on the baking sheet for the second time and put in the oven for an additional 20-25 minutes, or until pieces become brown and crispy.

Let cool for 5 minutes.

Q2 Favorite: Serve with cool celery and carrot sticks. Smash ¼ cup of bleu cheese crumbles and blend well with ¼ cup of plain Greek yogurt for a quick Bleu Cheese Dip.

Serves 4.

Q2: 100 calories per serving, protein: 2.6g, carbohydrates: 19.9g, fat: 1.3g, fiber 2.2g

Bleu Cheese Dip: 42 calories per serving, protein: 3.3g, carbohydrates: 1.1g, fat: 3g, fiber 0.3g

MOROCCAN MINI PEPPERS W/QUINOA

- 15 tri-colored peppers, baby bell (to fill)
- 1 cup quinoa, cooked – approximately ½ cup uncooked
- 1 fresh lemon
- ½ t. paprika
- ½ t. cumin
- ½ t. turmeric
- ¼ t. fine-grain sea salt
- Dash of cayenne pepper
- Fresh parsley, chopped for garnish

Q2 Tip: Use a vegetable steamer vs. boiling water to soften the peppers and retain the nutrients.

Cook the quinoa 1 minute less than the directions on the package and take the lid off immediately to keep the structure of the quinoa – soggy quinoa is less appealing.

1. Cut peppers in half, seed and clean. Place peppers in a vegetable steamer until slightly soft. Move peppers to a plate ready to fill.
2. Squeeze one lemon on the cooked quinoa. Blend the paprika, cumin, turmeric and salt together then mix to the quinoa.
3. Scoop the quinoa mixture into the peppers. Sprinkle with fresh parsley.

Makes 30.

Q2: 14 calories per pepper, protein: 0.5g, carbohydrates: 2.7g, fat: 0.2g, fiber 0.4g

QUINOA CRAB BALLS

- ½ cup quinoa, cooked and completely drained
- 8 oz. lump crab, fresh preferred
- ¼ cup red bell pepper, finely chopped
- ¼ cup celery, finely chopped
- ¼ cup green onions, finely chopped
- ½ t. kosher salt
- 1 egg white

Spice Mixture:
- ½ t. paprika
- ½ t. black pepper
- ¼ t. thyme
- 1/8 t. cayenne pepper

Combine in a small bowl and set aside.

Yogurt Mixture:
- ½ cup plain Greek yogurt, 0%
- ¼ cup olive oil or avocado mayonnaise
- ¼ cup sweet pickles, chopped
- 1 t. Dijon mustard

Combine in a separate bowl and set aside.

Q2 Tip: Refrigerate the crab balls on a parchment-lined plate for at least an hour before broiling.

1. Place crab in a medium bowl; mash slightly. Add quinoa, the spice mixture and half of the yogurt mixture – set aside the other half of the yogurt mixture to use as a dip.

2. Mix the red bell pepper, celery, green onions, kosher salt and egg white into the crab mixture and stir gently.

3. Roll into 1" round balls and place in the refrigerator on parchment paper for one hour.

Broil crab balls in lightly greased pan for 5 minutes or until slightly brown. Turn balls over and broil another 5 minutes or until brown. Serve with the yogurt dip or the Lemon Dipping Sauce on page 160

Makes 24.

Q2: 44 calories per ball, protein: 4.4g, carbohydrates: 5.3g, fat: 0.6g, fiber 0.6g

Yogurt dip: 30 calories per serving, protein: 0.5g, carbohydrates: 0.3g, fat: 3.2g, fiber 0.1g

SWEET POTATO NACHOS

- 2 lb. sweet potatoes, about 3-4 medium
- 1 T. avocado oil
- 2 t. paprika
- 1 t. garlic powder
- ½ t. cayenne pepper
- ½ cup black beans
- ½ cup tomatoes, chopped
- ½ cup avocado, chopped
- ½ cup cheddar cheese, shredded

Q2 Tip: Prepare two baking sheets for ultimate crispness. Lightly grease the baking sheet with avocado oil. Preheat oven to 425 degrees.

1. Peel and slice the sweet potatoes thin to about a quarter of an inch round.

2. Mix the oil, paprika, garlic powder and cayenne pepper in a large bowl.

   Toss the rounds in the oil mixture and place in a single layer on the baking sheets.

3. Bake for 10 minutes then carefully flip the sweet potatoes, and bake for an additional 10 minutes. Remove the pan from the oven and sprinkle the beans and cheese over the rounds.

Return to the oven until the cheese melts, about 2 minutes. Sprinkle with fresh tomato and avocado.

Serves 6.

Q2: 223 calories per serving, protein: 8.1g, carbohydrates: 31.5g, fat: 8g, fiber 7.6

Sweet Potato Nachos

SALADS

Chicory Salad with Berries - Page 175

Festive Kale Salad - Page 179

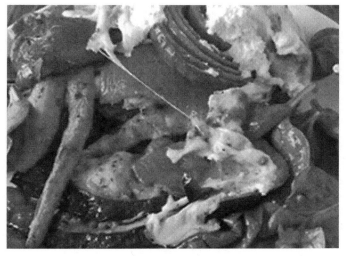

Grilled Veggie and Toasted Goat Cheese Spinach Salad - Page 182

171

AVOCADO ARUGULA QUINOA SALAD

- 5 oz. arugula (approximately 4 cups)
- 2 ripe avocados, peeled, pitted and diced
- ½ cup red bell pepper, chopped
- ½ cup celery, chopped
- 1 cup quinoa, cooked (approximately ½ cup dry quinoa to 1 cup of water)
- Fine-grain sea salt, to taste
- Ground black pepper, to taste

Q2 Tip: You can prepare the avocado quinoa ahead of time and add the arugula when ready to eat or serve.

One Step: Combine avocados, red pepper, celery and quinoa in a large bowl. Squeeze one lemon on top and toss gently. Refrigerate until ready to use or toss with arugula and season with salt and pepper to your liking.

Serves 4.

Q2: 238 calories per serving, protein: 5.9g, carbohydrates: 23.9g, fat: 14.9g, fiber 8.3g

BEET KALE SALAD

- Beet Kale Base Recipe on page 147 (kale, quinoa, walnuts, beets):
- 1 cup kale, chopped finely
- 1 lb. beets, cooked (approximately 4 pre-packaged cooked beets)
- 1 cup of cooked quinoa, approximately ½ cup of uncooked quinoa
- ¾ cup walnuts, chopped

- 5 oz. kale, chopped to consistency of your liking (approximately 4 cups)
- Asparagus tips
- 1/2 cup goat cheese, crumbled
- Balsamic vinegar, to taste
- Fine-grain sea salt, to taste
- Ground black pepper, to taste

Q2 Tip: Make the base recipe and enjoy this salad along with the Beet Breakfast Muffins on page 147 or Beet Burgers on page 217.

One Step: Combine all ingredients in a large bowl and toss with balsamic vinegar, salt and pepper, to taste.

Serves 4.

Q2: 322 calories per serving, protein: 13g, carbohydrates: 28.5g, fat: 17.8g, fiber 6.4

CHICORY SALAD W/APPLE CIDER DRESSING

- 1 T. shallot, minced
- ½ t. fine-grain sea salt
- 1 T. pure honey
- 3 T. apple cider vinegar
- Ground black pepper, dash
- 2-3 T. extra-virgin olive oil
- 5 oz. chicories (escarole, radicchio, endive, frisee)
- ¾ cup cucumber, peeled and diced
- ½ cup carrot, shredded
- 8 oz. cherry tomatoes
- ½ cup sunflower seeds

Q2 Tip: Toss with half of the vinaigrette as you can always add more.

1. Whisk the shallot, salt, honey, vinegar and pepper in a small mixing bowl, blend well. Add 2 T. of the olive oil, blend well. Taste and add an additional tablespoon to your liking.

2. Combine the chicories, cucumber, carrot and tomato in a large bowl. Toss with the vinaigrette and sunflower seeds.

Serves 2.

Q2: 280 calories per serving, protein: 4.9g, carbohydrates: 22.8g, fat: 20.3g, fiber 5.4g

CHICORY SALAD W/BERRIES

- 5 oz. chicories (escarole, radicchio, endive, frisee)
- 1 cup Brussel sprouts, shaved or sliced
- ¼ cup quinoa, uncooked
- ¼ cup black rice, uncooked
- 2 fresh lemons, juiced
- Fine-grain sea salt, to taste
- Ground black pepper, to taste
- 1 cup raspberries
- 1 cup blueberries
- ¼ cup pumpkin seeds

Q2 Tip: Have the cooked quinoa and black rice readily available then simply add ½ cup of cooked quinoa and ½ cup cooked black rice – and proceed to step 2.

1. Cook quinoa and black rice according to the package – ½ cup of water and ¼ cup quinoa in one saucepan and ½ cup of water and ¼ cup black rice in another saucepan. Remove the lids one minute prior to finish, let cool.

2. Combine the chicories, Brussel sprouts, quinoa and black rice in a large bowl. Squeeze with fresh lemon and toss. Season with salt and pepper to taste.

3. Toss in the raspberries, blueberries and pumpkin seeds. Serve with extra lemon wedges.

Serves 2.

Q2: 332 calories per serving, protein: 11.6g, carbohydrates: 54.3g, fat: 10.6g, fiber 12.9g

CRAB BALL SALAD

- 10 oz. mixed greens - spring mix works well
- 1 cup tri-color bell peppers, chopped or sliced
- 1 cup asparagus, grilled
- 1 cup black beans
- 1 T. white balsamic vinegar
- 1 fresh lemon, juiced
- Fine-grain sea salt, to taste
- Ground or coarse black pepper, to taste

Q2 Tip: Follow the recipe for Crab Balls on page 167. The Yogurt Dip is optional.

One Step: In a large bowl combine mixed greens, peppers, asparagus, white vinegar, lemon, salt and pepper. Place crab rolls on top of the salad and sprinkle with black beans. Serve with the yogurt dip on the side, if you wish, or the lemon dipping sauce on page 160

Serves 4.

Q2: 227 calories per salad/serving, protein: 13.5g, carbohydrates: 43.2g, fat: 0.9g, fiber 11.9g

Plus - Q2: 44 calories per crab ball, protein: 4.4g, carbohydrates: 5.3g, fat: 0.6g, fiber 0.6g

CREAMY APPLE/NUT SALAD

- 3/4 cup of the Goat Cheese Guacamole dip recipe on page 155
- 5 oz. spring mix (approximately 4 cups)
- 1 red apple, large, cut in small chunks
- 1 green apple, large, cut in small chunks
- ¾ cup walnuts or pecans cut in half or slightly chopped
- Fine-grain sea salt, to taste
- Ground black pepper, to taste

Q2 Tip: Use the remainder of the goat cheese guacamole recipe during the week for a healthy snack.

1. Thin the goat cheese dip with 2-3 T. of extra virgin olive oil, to your desired consistency.
2. Combine spring mix, apples and nuts in a large bowl.
3. Toss with Goat Cheese dressing. Add salt and pepper to your liking.

Serves 4.

Q2: 343 calories per serving, protein: 9.5g, carbohydrates: 19g, fat: 26.2g, fiber 6.7

QUICK FRUIT & NUT KALE SALAD

- 5 oz. kale, coarsely chopped (approximately 4 cups)
- 1 T. white balsamic vinegar
- 1 large apple or pear, cut into small chunks
- Seeds, nuts and dried fruit, of your choice

Q2 Favorite: 1/8 cup of each; pumpkin & sunflower seeds, slivered almonds and diced Figs.

One Step Meal: Toss all ingredients in a large bowl and enjoy!

Serves 2.

Q2: 274 calories per serving w/ Q2 Favorite, protein: 9.1g, carbohydrates: 36.4g, fat: 13.3g, fiber 7.6g

Fruit & Nut Kale Salad

FESTIVE KALE SALAD

- 10 oz. kale, coarsely chopped (approximately 8 cups)
- 8 oz. cherry tomatoes, sliced lengthwise in half
- ½ cup tri-color bell peppers, diced
- ½ cup cucumber, diced
- ¼ cup red onion, diced
- 2 garlic cloves, peeled
- ½ cup quinoa, uncooked
- ½ cup black rice, uncooked
- 2 fresh lemons, squeezed (approximately 1/8 cup)
- 2 T. balsamic vinegar
- Fine-grain sea salt, to taste
- Black pepper, to taste

Q2 Tip: Have the quinoa and black rice pre-made for the week and use 1 cup of cooked quinoa and 1 cup of cooked black rice for the salad. Season the salad with 1 t. garlic powder vs. smashed garlic clove for the quinoa and rice. (See step 1 below)

1. Cook quinoa and black rice according to the package – 1 cup of water and ½ cup quinoa in one saucepan and 1 cup of water and ½ cup black rice in another saucepan, adding one smashed garlic clove in each pot for flavor. Remove the lid one minute prior to finish, let cool and remove remaining garlic clove from each pot.

2. Wash the kale and thoroughly squeeze out the excess water using a salad spinner.

3. Toss all ingredients in a large bowl. Chill until ready to serve or eat.

Q2 Option: **Mediterranean Kale Salad**: Add ½ cup diced Olives and ½ cup Feta Cheese.

Serves 4.

Q2: 264 calories per serving, protein: 12.8g, carbohydrates: 49.7g, fat: 1.8g, fiber 6.2

QUICK WEDGE SALAD

- 1 head lettuce (Boston or butter)
- 1 large tomato cut in 8 wedges OR 8 cherry tomatoes
- 1 cucumber, cut into 1/8" round slices
- Extra virgin olive oil, to taste
- Balsamic vinegar, to taste
- Fine-grain sea salt, to taste
- Ground black pepper, to taste
- Garlic powder, to taste
- Dried oregano, to taste

Q2 Tip: This wedge salad is best served when chilled in the refrigerator before eating.

1. Cut off the stem of the lettuce then cut the lettuce into four wedges.

2. Wash and squeeze out excess water carefully and thoroughly. Place two tomatoes and six cucumbers around the wedge.

3. Drizzle each wedge with a little olive oil and balsamic vinegar and season each wedge with preferred spices; sea salt, black pepper, garlic powder, dried oregano and/or others of your choice.

Options: Add various vegetables, olives, cheese, etc. Get creative!

Makes 4 wedge salads.

Q2: 61 calories per wedge, protein: 1.7g, carbohydrates: 9.4g, fat: 2.8g, fiber 2g

RE-INVENTED HAWAIIAN SALAD

- 1 cup chopped oranges, seedless
- 1 cup pineapple, fresh and chopped
- 5 oz. plain Greek yogurt, 0%
- 5 oz. vanilla Greek yogurt, 0%
- 1 cup unsweetened coconut flakes

Option: Add pure honey for additional sweetness, to your liking.

Q2 Tip: Drain the juices of the fruit so that the salad does not become watery.

One Step: Combine all ingredients in a bowl and blend well.

Q2 Recommendation: Refrigerate for at least one hour before serving.

Serves 4.

Q2: 174 calories per serving, protein: 8.9g, carbohydrates: 21.7, fat: 6.9g, fiber 3.7g

GRILLED VEGGIE AND
TOASTED GOAT CHEESE SPINACH SALAD

- 5 oz. baby spinach (about 4 cups)
- 1 red pepper, seeded and cut lengthwise in half
- 1 green pepper, seeded and cut lengthwise in half
- 1 spanish onion, cut in ¼" round slices
- 1 large zucchini, trimmed and cut lengthwise in ¼" thickness
- 1 portabella mushroom
- 2 thin carrots, trimmed and peeled
- 1 T. balsamic vinegar
- 5 oz. ball of goat cheese
- Fine-grain sea salt, to taste
- Ground black pepper, to taste
- Avocado oil, to grease

Q2 Tip: Grill the veggies on a pre-heated and slightly greased grill top with avocado oil or cook in the oven at 400 degrees on a slightly greased crisper pan.

1. Season the veggies with a light sprinkle of salt and black pepper while on the grill top or before you put in oven. Cook until soft or slightly brown. Flip over and continue cooking to the consistency of your choice and grill marks.

2. Toast the goat cheese ball in a 400-degree oven on a parchment-paper-lined pan for 3-5 minutes or until golden brown. Remove from oven.

3. Mix the baby spinach and balsamic vinegar to coat lightly in a large serving bowl. Arrange the grilled vegetables on the bed of spinach and place the goat cheese in the center.

Serves 2.

Q2: 324 calories per serving, protein: 20g, carbohydrates: 30.5g, fat: 15.9g, fiber 8.9g

Quick Chicken Salad – See recipe on Page 244

Grilled Veggie and Toasted Goat Cheese Spinach Salad

SOUPS

Miso Broth w Rice Noodles - Page 190   Pasta Fagioli Remix - Page 192

Fall Harvest Soup - Page 188

COLLARD GREEN SOUP

- 5 oz. collard greens (about 4 cups), stems removed and cut into large pieces
- 8 oz. mushrooms, trimmed, cleaned and sliced
- 4 green onions, white and pale green parts, cleaned and sliced
- Pinch of red pepper flakes
- 1 cup vegetable stock or chicken stock, organic – zero to low-sodium
- 1 parsnip, peeled and cubed
- 1 turnip, peeled and cubed
- ½ cup uncooked quinoa
- 4 cups water
- 2 cups fresh baby peas
- 2 fresh lemons, juiced
- Fine-grain sea salt, to taste
- Ground black pepper, to taste
- Olive oil, to sauté

Optional: Plain Greek yogurt, lemon zest, tomato and/or coarse black pepper for garnish.

Q2 Tip: To use parsnip and turnip, scrub clean and gently remove the skin with a vegetable peeler until the peel is thoroughly removed. Clean again before cutting into cubes.

1. Heat oil in a saucepan over medium heat. Add the mushrooms and cook until soft, about 5 minutes. Add green onion and cook until tender, about 4 minutes. Add red pepper flakes, stir, and immediately add the vegetable stock. Bring to a slight boil.

2. Add the parsnip and turnip, quinoa and 4 cups of water; bring to a boil then a simmer, about 15 minutes. Add peas and collards, stir occasionally, 3 minutes. Cool for 10 minutes.

3. Transfer cooled mixture to a blender and process until smooth. Return mixture to saucepan, simmer over low heat. Remove from heat and stir in lemon juice. Season to taste with salt and pepper.

Ladle soup into bowls and garnish with a dollop of plain Greek yogurt, lemon zest, tomato and/or course black pepper.

Serves 4.

Q2: 206 calories per serving, protein: 10.8g, carbohydrates: 36.3g, fat: 2g, fiber 10.9

FALL HARVEST SOUP

- 1 large kabocha squash, about 6 lbs. (can substitute butternut squash)
- 1 t. cinnamon
- ½ t. fine-grain sea salt
- ¼ t. red pepper flakes
- ¼ t. nutmeg
- 3 T. olive oil (divided, 1 T. + 2 T.)
- ¾ cup yellow onion, chopped
- 1 shallot, finely chopped
- 1 t. ginger root, minced
- 1 Fuji apple, peeled, cored and chopped into ½-inch cubes
- 2 pears, peeled, cored and chopped into ½-inch cubes
- 32 oz. vegetable stock, organic – zero to low-sodium

Optional: Pumpkin seeds for garnish, crunch and flavor

Q2 Tip: Cook the squash prior to making the soup – step 1 – in a preheated oven of 425 degrees.

1. Whisk cinnamon, salt, red pepper flakes, nutmeg and 1 T. olive oil in a small bowl. Brush inside flesh of squash with the spice mixture, reserving any remaining. Line a baking pan with parchment paper and lay the squash cut side down. Roast for 30-40 minutes at 425 degrees or until very soft. Remove from oven and let cool.

2. Meanwhile, heat the remaining 2 T. of the olive oil and the reserved spice mixture in a stockpot over medium heat. Add onions and a pinch of salt; cook until onions are soft, about

2 minutes. Add shallots and sauté for about 3 minutes. Add ginger, pears and apple; sauté for 3-5 minute or until the fruit softens and turns golden brown. Add the vegetable stock to blend well then simmer for 10 minutes.

3. Scoop out the flesh of the cooled squash and transfer to the pot. Mash the squash gently into the soup, add the pumpkin, and continue to mash, stir and blend well. Use an immersion blender for a creamier soup or mash to consistency of your liking. Simmer for 10 minutes.

Ladle soup into bowls and garnish with pumpkin seed.

Serves 4.

Q2: 231 calories per serving, protein: 3.7g, carbohydrates: 33.8g, fat: 11.4g, fiber 8.3g

MISO BROTH W/RICE NOODLES

- 1 T. avocado oil
- 2 t. ginger root, freshly grated
- 3 garlic cloves, minced
- 32 oz. vegetable stock, organic – zero to low-sodium
- 1 cup water
- 8 dried shiitake mushrooms
- 3 T. bonita miso
- 1 T. liquid aminos (can substitute low-sodium soy sauce)
- ½ lb. rice noodles*
- 1 cup white mushrooms, thinly sliced
- 2 carrots, cut in thin 1-inch shreds or matchsticks
- ½ cup peas

Optional: Hard-boiled egg, hot sauce, green onions

Q2 Tip: *This broth pairs well with rice noodles, but you can change it up and use chickpea or quinoa noodles, black or brown rice and add a variety of vegetables, to your liking.

1. Heat oil in a large saucepan over medium heat. Add the ginger and garlic, stir and cook for 2 minutes. Slowly add broth and water, bring to a simmer. Add dried shiitake mushrooms, simmer for 5 minutes. Whisk miso and liquid aminos in a small bowl then gradually whisk into the broth. Simmer for 5 minutes.

2. Cook the noodles according to package directions.

3. Meanwhile, add mushrooms, carrots and peas to the broth. Simmer for 10 minutes until vegetables are slightly softened.

Ladle soup into bowls and garnish with an open faced hard-boiled egg (cut in half lengthwise). Flavor it up with green onions and/or spice it up with hot sauce.

Serves 4.

Q2: 233 calories per serving, protein: 8.7g, carbohydrates: 46.8g, fat: 2.9g, fiber 7.5g

Add a hard-boiled egg for 60 extra calories and an extra 5g of protein.

PASTA FAGIOLI REMIX

- 1 T. olive oil
- 1 cup yellow onion, finely chopped
- Pinch of fine-grain sea salt
- 1 ½ cups carrots*, peeled and chopped into rounds
- 1 ½ cups zucchini, peeled and diced
- 1 garlic clove
- 1 t. oregano, fresh or dried
- 1 t. thyme, fresh or dried
- ½ t. fine-grain sea salt
- ½ t. ground black pepper
- Pinch of red pepper flakes
- ½ lb. quinoa or chickpea pasta, medium shells or bows
- 32 oz. vegetable stock, organic – zero to low-sodium
- 8 campari or plum tomatoes, pulsed
- 1 15-ounce can light red kidney beans, rinsed and drained
- 1 15-ounce can cannellini beans, rinsed and drained
- 2 cups Swiss chard, stemmed and finely chopped

Optional: Fresh parmesan cheese and black pepper

Q2 Tip: *Add color and flavor to your dish – use multi-colored carrots; orange, yellow and purple.

1. Heat oil in a large stockpot over medium heat. Add onion and a pinch of salt, stir and cook for 2 minutes. Add carrots, zucchini, garlic, oregano, thyme, black pepper, salt and red pepper flakes. Cook and stir for about 10 minutes.

2. Cook the noodles according to package directions.

3. Meanwhile, add the broth, tomatoes and beans. Bring to a boil, then reduce heat to a simmer. Stir in Swiss chard. Cover and simmer for 20 minutes. Stir in cooked pasta.

Ladle soup into bowls and garnish with fresh parmesan cheese.

Q2: 380 calories per serving, protein: 28.1g, carbohydrates: 68.7g, fat: 4.7g, fiber 10.3g

SLOW COOKED TOMATO BEAN BARLEY (MULTI-BEAN OR LENTIL SOUP)

- 2 cups of dried beans (multi-bean or just lentils)
- 32 oz. vegetable stock, organic – zero to low-sodium
- 1 cup pearl barley
- 12 heirloom tomatoes, medium sized, cut in quarters
- ½ cup carrots, chopped
- 1 onion, medium sized, chopped
- 1 t. fresh garlic, minced
- 1 t. basil
- 1 t. thyme
- ½ t. cumin
- ½ t. fine-grain sea salt
- ½ t. ground black pepper

Q2 Tip: Sort through the dried beans on a cookie sheet to make sure no debris, stones or rocks exist, then soak and rinse the beans in cold water at least three times. Ideally, sort, rinse and then soak overnight.

One Step: Combine all ingredients in the crockpot and slow cook on low for eight hours or on high heat for five hours.

Serves 4.

Q2: 292 calories per serving, protein: 10.7g, carbohydrates: 63.3g, fat: 1.7g, fiber 16.3

SWEET POTATO SOUP

- 3 lbs. sweet potatoes, peeled
- 1 medium red onion, chopped
- 1 T. fresh ginger root, chopped
- Pinch of red pepper flakes
- 32 oz. vegetable stock or chicken stock, organic – zero to low-sodium
- 1 cup coconut milk, 100% - unsweetened
- 1 T. 100% pure honey
- 1 t. cinnamon
- 1 T. olive oil, to sauté

Optional: Pumpkin seeds, garnish

Q2 Tip: Use fresh ginger root, gently remove the skin with a peeler until the white ginger is visible; cut a chunk out and chop.

1. Heat oil in a saucepan over medium heat. Add red onion and ginger and cook until soft, about 5 minutes. Add red pepper flakes, stir, and immediately add the vegetable stock. Bring to a slight boil.

2. Add sweet potatoes; bring to a simmer. Cook until potatoes are soft, about 25 minutes. Cool for 15 minutes.

3. Transfer cooled mixture to a blender and process until smooth. Return mixture to saucepan, simmer over low heat. Whisk in coconut milk, honey and cinnamon. Cook until thickened and hot – ready to serve.

Ladle soup into bowls and place a spoonful of pumpkin seeds in the center for garnish, extra crunch and flavor.

Serves 8.

Q2: 321 calories per serving, protein: 3.9g, carbohydrates: 58.1g, fat: 9.3g, fiber 8.7

VEGETABLE CURRY

- 1 T. olive oil
- 1 ½ cups sweet potatoes, peeled and diced
- 1 ½ cups cauliflower*, cut into florets
- 1/3 cup yellow onion, sliced thin
- 3 t. curry powder
- 1 ½ cups vegetable stock, organic – zero to low-sodium
- ½ cup water
- ½ t. fine-grain sea salt
- 15 oz. garbanzo beans (chickpeas), rinsed and drained
- 4 campari or plum tomatoes, chopped

Optional: Plain Greek yogurt, coarse black pepper and fresh parsley

Q2 Tip: *Add color and flavor to your dish – substitute cauliflower with purple cauliflower.

1. Heat oil in a large saucepan over medium heat. Add sweet potatoes and sauté for 5 minutes.
2. Add cauliflower, onion and curry powder, stir and cook for 2 minutes.
3. Add broth, water, salt, garbanzo beans and tomatoes. Bring to a boil, then simmer for 10 minutes until vegetables are slightly softened.

Ladle soup into bowls and serve with a dollop of yogurt, coarse pepper and parsley.

Serves 4.

Q2: 250 calories per serving, protein: 9.2g, carbohydrates: 43.5g, fat: 5.8g, fiber 10.1g

PIZZA & PASTA

Harvest Polenta Pizza Pie - Page 203   Cauliflower Crust Pizza - Page 198

Green Creamy Quinoa Pasta with Roasted Tomatoes - Page 204

BROCCOLI OR CAULIFLOWER CRUST PIZZA PIE

- 1 small head of broccoli OR 1 small head of cauliflower (about 1 ½ lbs.)
- ½ cup parmesan cheese, fresh and grated
- ½ cup ground oats
- 1 egg + 1 egg white, whisked
- 1 garlic clove, fresh and chopped
- 1 T. basil, fresh and chopped
- ¼ t. fine-grain sea salt
- ¼ t. ground black pepper
- 1 Recipe for Simple Pizza Sauce (See recipe page 200)

Q2 Tip: If you incorporate meat or chicken for the topping, pre-cook beforehand.

1. Make broccoli or cauliflower rice by pulsing a handful at a time in a food processor until it looks like grains of rice.

2. In a saucepan, fill with water to right below the steamer insert. Bring water to a boil. Add the broccoli or cauliflower and steam for 15 minutes. Remove from heat, press out excess water and transfer to a bowl. Refrigerate for 10 minutes, stir, refrigerate for another 10 minutes.

3. In a large bowl, combine the cheese, oats, eggs, garlic, basil, salt and pepper – mix well. Fold in the vegetable rice mixture and continue to blend well. Line a baking sheet with parchment paper. Spread, press and shape the crust, to your liking.

Bake: 425 degrees until lightly browned, about 15-20 minutes. Remove the pan from the oven and top the pizza with sauce, cheese, and/or toppings of your choice. Bake for another 5-8 minutes.

Q2 Favorite: Spread Simple Pizza Sauce on pre-cooked crust, top it with cooked quinoa, diced Kale, fresh garlic and giardiniera. Bake for 5 minutes.

Q2: 452 calories per one large crust, protein: 35.6g, carbohydrates: 48.5g, fat: 14.6g, fiber 11.3g

EASY MARINARA PIZZA AND PASTA SAUCE

- 28 oz. crushed tomatoes
- 2 garlic cloves, chopped
- 1 bay leaf
- ¾ t. fine-grain sea salt
- ½ t. ground black pepper
- 2 T. parmesan cheese, fresh grated
- 2 T. fresh basil, chopped

Q2 Tip: Add basil and parmesan during the last 5 minutes of cooking for flavor and to thicken.

1. Combine pureed tomatoes, garlic, bay leaf, salt and black pepper and bring to a slight boil.
2. Reduce heat and simmer for 20 minutes.
3. Add parmesan cheese and basil and stir consistently. Simmer for 5 minutes then remove from heat.

Use as a condiment, on your favorite pizza or as a sauce on your pasta and vegetable noodles.

Serves 8.

Q2: 64 calories per recipe, protein: 4.7g, carbohydrates: 8.6g, fat: 1.5g, fiber 3.3g

EGGPLANT PARMIGIANA POLENTA PIZZA PIE

- 1 1/2 cups instant polenta
- 4 1/2 cups water
- 1 t. fine-grain sea salt
- 1 recipe of Easy Marinara Pizza and Pasta Sauce on page 200
- 2 eggplant, large, peeled and sliced ¼" thick in diameter
- ¼ cup parmesan cheese, fresh
- ½ t. garlic powder
- 8 oz. mozzarella, fresh – crumbled
- Ground black pepper, to taste
- Fresh parmesan cheese, to taste

Q2 Tip: The key to making polenta is to stir it consistently while cooking so that it does not clump, and then use it immediately so that it is easy to spread.

1. Cook the polenta according to the directions on the package. Spoon and press the polenta on a slightly oiled 10x15 baking pan. Let cool.

2. Spread a layer of the pizza sauce on top of the polenta. Combine the eggplant slices, parmesan cheese, garlic powder and one cup of the pizza sauce in a large bowl, toss and blend well. Arrange the eggplant slices in a row building up any extra spaces on top. Toss crumbled mozzarella on top along with any remaining sauce/parmesan when tossed with the eggplant.

3. Sprinkle with black pepper and additional parmesan cheese and put in the oven.

Bake: 375 degrees for 25-30 minutes or until lightly browned and the crust has hardened. Take out of the oven and let it set about 15-20 minutes before cutting. Sprinkle with fresh basil before serving. The crust will remain slightly soft, but you should be able to eat it with your hands, if you would like.

Q2 Recommendation: Reserve the remaining sauce to be used during the week as a condiment or to create mini-polenta pizzas in a ramekin with your favorite toppings.

Serves 8 or Makes 16 appetizer squares.

Q2: 196 calories per serving, protein: 13.4g, carbohydrates: 25.2g, fat: 6.4g, fiber 7.6g

Appetizer: 98 calories per square, protein: 6.7g, carbohydrates: 12.6g, fat: 3.2g, fiber 3.8g

Eggplant Parmigiana Polenta Pizza Pie

HARVEST POLENTA PIZZA PIE

- 1 cup instant polenta
- 3 cups water
- ¾ t. fine-grain sea salt
- 1 lb. ricotta cheese, fresh
- 1 squash, peeled and sliced ¼" thick in diameter
- 1 zucchini, peeled and sliced ¼" thick in diameter
- 2 campari tomatoes, sliced ¼" thick in diameter
- Ground black pepper, to taste

Q2 Tip: The key to making polenta is to stir it consistently while cooking so that it does not clump and then use it immediately so that it is easy to spread.

1. Cook the polenta according to the directions on the package. Spoon and press the polenta on a slightly oiled 8x8 baking pan. Let cool.
2. Spread the ricotta cheese on top of the polenta. Place the vegetable slices in a row so that when you cut into squares, each piece will have a vegetable.
3. Sprinkle with black pepper and put in the oven.

Bake: 375 degrees for 20-25 minutes or until lightly browned and the crust has hardened. Let it set about 15 minutes before cutting and serving. The crust will remain slightly soft, but you should be able to eat it with your hands, if you would like.

Serves 6 or makes 12 appetizer squares.

Q2: 139 calories per serving, protein: 10g, carbohydrates: 11.3g, fat: 6.2g, fiber 1.3g

Appetizer: 69 calories per square, protein: 5g, carbohydrates: 5.6g, fat: 3.1g, fiber 0.6g

Q2 Favorite: Spread Ricotta Cheese on crust and bake for 5 minutes. Top with arugula, fresh tomato slices, pine nuts and basil and put in the oven for an additional 3 minutes. Drizzle with balsamic vinegar. Makes one large crust or various small pizzas.

GREEN CREAMY QUINOA PASTA W/ROASTED TOMATOES

- 1 Recipe of Avocado Hummus (page 151)
- 14 oz. quinoa pasta, shells or other
- 8 campari tomatoes (or compared to a little larger than a cherry tomato)

Optional: Fresh parmesan cheese, to taste

Q2 Tip: Make the Avocado Hummus ahead of time. For a thinner pasta sauce, add 1 t. olive oil and 1 t. water and blend well.

1. Cook pasta according to the directions on the package.
2. Cut tomatoes in half and put on a slightly greased baking pan. Sprinkle or spray each tomato with oil and pepper. Place under the broiler until slightly brown, about 6-8 minutes.
3. In the meantime, drain the pasta and toss with Avocado Hummus Sauce. Stir in fresh baby spinach and feta cheese to your liking and serve with tossed roasted tomatoes.

Serves 6.

Q2: 368 calories per serving, protein: 19.1g, carbohydrates: 54.8g, fat: 9.9g, fiber 22g

ROASTED SPAGHETTI SQUASH

- 4 lbs. spaghetti squash, cut in half lengthwise
- 1 T. olive oil
- Fine-grain sea salt, to taste
- Ground black pepper, to taste

Optional: 1 recipe of Easy Marinara Pizza and Pasta Sauce on page 200 or Roasted Red Pepper Sauce on page 206 – see below.

Q2 Tip: Cook the squash prior to making the soup – step 1 – in a preheated oven of 425 degrees.

1. Scoop out the seeds and connecting strands of the squash, then place cut side down on a baking pan lined with parchment paper.
2. Roast for 30-40 minutes at 425 degrees or until very soft. Remove from oven and let cool.
3. Turn the squash cut size up and loosen from the shells with a fork, making spaghetti strands.

Serve warm, with additional parmesan cheese and/or your favorite pasta sauce.

Q2: 173 calories per serving plain, protein: 2.9g, carbohydrates: 31.4g, fat: 6.1g, fiber 0.5g

ROASTED RED PEPPER SAUCE

- 12 campari or plum tomatoes
- 2 garlic cloves, chopped
- 1 bay leaf
- 2 large red peppers, roasted and finely chopped (can substitute jarred roasted peppers)
- 1/3 cup sun-dried tomatoes, finely chopped
- ½ t. fine-grain sea salt
- ½ t. ground black pepper
- 2 T. fresh basil, chopped
- 2 T. fresh parsley, chopped
- 2 T. parmesan cheese, fresh

Q2 Tip: Add fresh basil and parsley during the last 5 minutes of cooking for flavor. Remove from heat and add parmesan to thicken – add more for consistency desired. Roast peppers in the oven on parchment paper for 30 minutes at 400 degrees or use jarred roasted peppers for convenience.

1. Puree tomatoes in a food processor. Set aside.
2. Combine pureed tomatoes, garlic, red pepper flakes, sun-dried tomatoes, roasted pepper, bay leaf, salt and black pepper and bring to a slight boil. Reduce heat immediately and simmer for 20 minutes. Add basil and parsley and simmer for another 5 minutes.
3. Remove from heat and add parmesan cheese.

Use as a condiment, on your favorite pizza or as a sauce on your pasta and vegetable noodles.

Serves 8.

Q2: 67 calories per serving, protein: 3.8g, carbohydrates: 12.6g, fat: 1.2g, fiber 2.6g

ZUCCHINI NOODLES

- 6 lbs. zucchini, washed with skin left on or peeled
- Easy Marinara Pizza and Pasta Sauce recipe on page 200 or Roasted Red Pepper Sauce (206).

Optional: Fresh parmesan cheese, to taste

Q2 Tip: A vegetable spiralizer works best, but you can use a hand spiralizer, apple corer/peeler/slicer, mandolin or even a potato peeler to create strings of zucchini pasta.

1. Cut off ends of the zucchini and spiral with your preference.
2. Place in vegetable steamer until just wilted. Remove immediately.
3. Place on a dish, add your marinara and enjoy!

Serves 4.

Q2: 109 calories per serving plain, protein: 8.2g, carbohydrates: 22.8g, fat: 1.2g, fiber 7.5g

Zucchini Noodles

VEGETABLES and MEATLESS MEALS

Baked Edamame Falafel – Page 215

Mushroom, Onion and Pea Risotto – Page 220

Tempeh Stir Fry – Page 224

Vegetarian Stuffed Peppers – Page 223

ARTICHOKE, SNOW PEAS, AND ASPARAGUS

- 2 T. extra-virgin olive oil
- 1 fresh lemon, juiced
- ½ t. oregano, dried
- ¼ t. fine-grain sea salt
- ¼ t. ground black pepper
- ½ lb. snow peas
- 1 lb. asparagus, tough ends removed and cut into 1-inch chunks
- 1-14 oz. can artichoke hearts, drained, rinsed and quartered

Optional: Lemon wedges, red pepper flakes

Q2 Tip: Want some heat? Add a pinch or two of red pepper flakes.

1. Whisk olive oil, lemon juice, oregano, garlic, salt and pepper in a large bowl.
2. Meanwhile, steam snow peas and asparagus until slightly tender. Remove from steamer and drain any excess water.
3. Combine the artichokes, snow peas and asparagus in the olive oil mixture and toss until fully covered.

Serve with a lemon wedge.

Serves 4.

Q2: 114 calories per serving, protein: 4.7g, carbohydrates: 10.3g, fat: 7.3g, fiber 4.7g

CREAMY LIME RICE

- 1 cup jasmine rice, rinsed under cold water per directions
- 1 cup coconut milk, 100% - unsweetened
- 1 cup water
- ¼ t. fine-grain sea salt
- 1 fresh lime, juiced
- 1 T. parsley, fresh or dried

Q2 Tip: Once this creamy rice is made, you can enjoy alone, with a meal or transform it by adding your favorite chopped vegetables, beans or seeds or spice - like turmeric or cilantro.

1. Combine rice, coconut milk, water and salt in a saucepan. Bring to a boil then reduce on medium-heat for about 10-12 minutes or until the liquid is absorbed.

2. Remove from the heat. Fluff with a fork, then move to a bowl with minimal stirring.

3. Top it off with lime juice and parsley and incorporate gently with a fork.

Q2 Favorite: Add sautéed red bell pepper and black beans for a festive creamy rice.

Makes 3 cups. Serves 6.

Q2: 124 calories per serving, protein: 2.9g, carbohydrates: 27.7g, fat: 0.1g, fiber 4g

Creamy Cauliflower Rice: Follow the same recipe as the Creamy Lime Rice - but substitute 3 cups of pulsed cauliflower rice for the jasmine rice and omit water.

HEALTHIER MASHED POTATOES

- 2 russet potatoes, large
- 1 lb. cauliflower florets
- 16 oz. cottage cheese, 2%
- ½ t. fine-grain sea salt
- ½ t. ground black pepper
- 1 t. garlic powder

Q2 Tip: Mix with flavors that you like – for instance, replace sea salt for onion salt, omit garlic and add grilled chopped onion for French Onion Mashed Potatoes.

1. Boil the potatoes and cauliflower in two separate slightly salted saucepans, until tender.
2. Combine the cottage cheese and tender cauliflower in a food processor – blend well. Pour into the bowl and place tender potatoes on top along with the salt, pepper and garlic powder.
3. Mash the potatoes into the mixture until consistency desired then fold to mix thoroughly.

Serves 6.

Q2: 138 calories per serving, protein: 13.2g, carbohydrates: 18.4g, fat: 1.6g, fiber 3.7g

ROASTED BRUSSELS SPROUTS AND SWEET POTATOES

- 4 cups of Brussels sprouts
- 2 large sweet potatoes, diced in 1-inch cubes
- 2 T. grapeseed or avocado oil
- 1 t. garlic powder
- 1 t. ground cumin
- ½ t. nutmeg
- ¾ t. fine-grain sea salt

Optional: ¼ cup raw pecans or walnuts, 1/3 cup feta cheese, ¼ cup balsamic vinegar

Q2 Tip: This recipe is ready to eat or accompany a meal without the options, or you can transform this dish with nuts OR feta cheese and balsamic vinegar option.

One Step: Toss Brussels sprouts, sweet potato, olive oil, garlic powder, cumin, nutmeg and sea salt in a large bowl, coat well then layer in a lightly greased baking pan.

Bake: 400 degrees for 50 minutes, stirring once halfway through.

Q2 Options: Remove from oven and douse with balsamic vinegar and feta cheese or add nuts during the last 5 minutes of cooking.

Serves 6.

Q2: 124 calories per serving, protein: 3.4g, carbohydrates: 27.1g, fat: 1.1g, fiber 5.6g

WHOLE ROASTED CAULIFLOWER

- 1 cauliflower head
- 3 T. coconut oil
- ¼ t. fine-grain sea salt
- 1/8 t. cinnamon
- 1/8 t. paprika
- 1/8 t. cumin or cayenne pepper (dependent on flavor)
- Ground black pepper, pinch

Q2 Tip: Try various other spices – this is a great healthy snack, for an appetizer or to accompany a meal.

1. Carefully remove leaves from the cauliflower head. Cut the stem so that it is flat yet stays intact. Place the cauliflower upright on a baking pan.
2. Melt the coconut oil and coat the cauliflower head thoroughly.
3. Combine the spices in a small bowl and gently sprinkle the spice mixture evenly on the cauliflower head.

Bake: 425 degrees for 40-45 minutes or until brown and tender

Serves 4.

Q2: 107 calories per serving, protein: 1.3g, carbohydrates: 3.6g, fat: 10.6g, fiber 1.7

Shepherd's Pie Remix: Use the Whole Roasted Cauliflower Recipe in place of the chicken.

Simply tear or cut the cooled cauliflower head and create a Vegetable Shepherd's Pie.

Or use Tempeh for another Vegetable Shephard's Pie option.

BAKED EDAMAME FALAFEL

- 16 oz. edamame, shelled
- 1 T. extra-virgin olive oil
- ½ cup panko, crunchy bread crumbs + ¼ cup additional
- ¼ t. paprika
- ¼ t. cumin
- ¼ t. turmeric
- ¼ t. fine-grain sea salt + 1/8 t. additional
- Dash of cinnamon
- Dash of cayenne pepper
- Grapeseed or avocado oil, to grease baking sheet
- Tzatziki Sauce recipe on page 159

Optional: Cucumber, tomatoes, lettuce, onions, lemon wedges (garnish for Falafel Sandwich)

Q2 Tip: Serve as an appetizer with the tzatziki sauce or as a meal with or without the naan bread - prep the fixings ahead; matchsticked or sliced cucumbers, tomatoes, lettuce, onions, lemon wedges.

1. Combine the ½ cup of bread crumbs and 1/8 teaspoon salt in a medium bowl, blend well and set aside.

2. Combine edamame, oil, paprika, cumin, turmeric, cinnamon, cayenne pepper, salt and 1/4 cup of the bread crumb mixture in a food processor – blend well, until pulsed into tiny pieces and somewhat smooth. Remove from the food processor and put in a separate bowl.

3. Form balls with the edamame mixture by rolling them in your hands, about 1" diameter. Then roll the formed balls in the

panko/salt mixture until fully coated. Repeat until all mixture is used. Place on a lightly greased baking sheet (grapeseed or avocado oil).

Bake: 400 degrees for 15 minutes, then gently flip the balls and cook for an additional 10 minutes or until golden brown. Serve as an appetizer or as a meal, with or without naan bread and with the fixings of a complete falafel sandwich.

Makes 28.

Q2: 30 calories per falafel, protein: 1.8g, carbohydrates: 2.8g, fat: 1.4g, fiber 0.6g

BEET BURGER

Beet Kale Base Recipe on page 147 (kale, quinoa, walnuts, beets):

- 1 cup kale, chopped finely
- 1 lb. beets, cooked (approximately 4 pre-packaged cooked beets)
- 1 cup of cooked quinoa, approximately ½ cup of uncooked quinoa
- ¾ cup walnuts, chopped (optional)

- ¾ cup panko, crunchy bread crumbs + ¼ cup additional
- ½ cup goat cheese, finely crumbled
- 1/8 t. fine-grain sea salt
- 1/8 t. ground black pepper

Q2 Tip: Make the base recipe and enjoy this recipe along with the Beet Breakfast Muffins on page 147 or Kale Beet Salad on page 173

1. Combine base recipe (kale, quinoa, walnuts, beets), ¾ cup of bread crumbs, goat cheese, salt and pepper in a large bowl – blend well by folding with spoon. Place ¼ cup of additional bread crumbs in a separate bowl, set aside.
2. Use your hands to form beet burger patties.
3. Gently flip the burgers in the additional bread crumbs to coat each side lightly. Place on a parchment-lined baking sheet.

Bake: 375 degrees for 10 minutes on each side – 20 minutes total.

Makes 6 burgers or 12 sliders.

Q2: 232 calories per burger, protein: 10.4g, carbohydrates: 23.2g, fat: 11.6g, fiber 3.8

Q2 Appetizer: 116 calories per slider, protein: 5.2g, carbohydrates: 11.6g, fat 5.8g, fiber 1.9g

BUTTERNUT SQUASH AND ZUCCHINI BOATS

- 2 large zucchini
- 2 large butternut squash
- Sauce of your liking:

For Italian Style:

- Easy Marinara (page 200)
- Quinoa
- Zucchini squash
- Tri-Colored baby bell peppers, chopped
- Onions, diced
- Organic tempeh

For Mexican Style:

- Homemade Salsa Verde (page 154)
- Rice (black, brown, basmati)
- Black beans
- Avocado, chopped
- Tomato, chopped
- Organic tempeh

Q2 Tip: You can make the boats in various sizes for a meal, snack or appetizers.

1. Cut the zucchini and/or squash in half lengthwise, carefully cut out or scoop the insides and put them to the side to use later. Place the boats in a steamer until slightly soft.

2. Remove from steamer and strain excess water, then place on a plate.

3. Pre-sauté your veggies and tempeh. Fill your boats according to Italian or Mexican style, serve or top with the Easy Marinara or Salsa Verde.

Q2 Recommendation: Try tempeh for a meatier meal along with a healthy dose of probiotic.

Makes 8 boats/serving. Can be cut in 2" mini-boats for an appetizer or a quick snack.

Q2 Italian: 148 calories per serving*, protein: 7.8g, carbohydrates: 22.8g, fat: 3.5g, fiber 3.2g

Q2 Mexican: 160 calories per serving*, protein: 6.8g, carbohydrates: 20.9g, fat 6.4g, fiber 4.7g

*The calculation is approximate using about 1-3 T. of each ingredient and without the sauce.

MUSHROOM, ONION AND PEA RISOTTO

- 2 T. olive oil
- 2 T. butter
- 2 shallots, thinly chopped
- ¼ cup Vidalia onion, thinly chopped
- 1 cup white mushrooms, chopped
- 1 cup baby bella mushrooms, chopped
- 6 garlic cloves, minced
- 2 cups arborio rice
- 32 oz. vegetable stock, organic - zero to low-sodium (warmed on the cooktop)
- 1 cup dry white wine
- Fine-grain sea salt, to taste
- Ground black pepper, to taste

Q2 Tip: This will take at least 30 minutes to completely cook, and you will need to be consistent in stirring constantly while adding parts of stock and wine.

1. Heat oil and butter in a large skillet pan. Sauté the shallots, onions and mushrooms for 3 minutes. Add the garlic and sauté for 2 minutes. Put rice in the pan and stir for 3 minutes or until it starts to lightly toast. Gradually add one cup of the stock and keep stirring until liquid is absorbed.

2. Add ¼ cup of the wine and keep stirring until absorbed. Add 1 cup of the stock and stir until absorbed. Continue this pattern until the remainder of the wine and stock are incorporated.

Add the frozen peas and stir for an additional 5 minutes or until warm through.

3. Season with salt and pepper to taste or add parmesan cheese.

Ready to eat or accompany a meal.

Q2 Transformation: Serve in steamed peppers with an Easy Marinara sauce on page 200

Serves 8.

Q2: 271 calories per serving, protein: 4.5g, carbohydrates: 42.4g, fat: 6.8g, fiber 2.3g

ROASTED RED PEPPER RISOTTO

- 2 T. olive oil
- 2 T. butter
- 2 shallots, thinly chopped
- 1 cup red bell pepper, chopped
- 6 garlic cloves, minced
- 2 cups arborio rice
- 32 oz. vegetable stock, organic - zero to low-sodium (warmed on the cooktop)
- 1 cup dry white wine
- Fine-grain sea salt, to taste
- Ground black pepper, to taste

Q2 Tip: It will take at least 30 minutes to completely cook and you will need to be consistent in stirring constantly while adding parts of stock and wine.

1. Heat oil and butter in a large skillet pan. Sauté the shallots, red pepper for 2 minutes. Add the garlic and sauté for 2 minutes. Put rice in the pan and stir for 3 minutes. Gradually add one cup of the stock and keep stirring until liquid is absorbed. It will take about 30 minutes to completely cook and you will need to be consistent in stirring while adding parts of stock and wine.

2. Add ¼ cup of the wine and keep stirring until absorbed. Add 1 cup of the stock and stir again until absorbed. Continue this pattern until the remainder of the wine and stock are incorporated.

3. Season with salt and pepper to taste or add parmesan cheese.

Q2 Transformation: Transform this risotto into Vegetarian Stuffed Bell Peppers on page 223

Serves 8.

Q2: 214 calories per serving, protein: 9.5g, carbohydrates: 29g, fat: 6.6g, fiber 0.8g

VEGETARIAN STUFFED PEPPERS

- 4 whole green or red Peppers, large
- 1 cup portabella mushrooms, diced
- 1 cup asparagus, cut into 1/2-inch pieces
- 1 cup baby spinach, chopped
- 1 cup recipe of Roasted Red Pepper Risotto
- 1/2 cup goat cheese
- ¾ cup sherry vinegar
- Balsamic vinegar, to taste

Q2 Tip: Ahead of time, make the Roasted Red Pepper Risotto on page 222 or use your favorite rice, barley or quinoa.

1. Steam the peppers in a vegetable steamer or stockpot until slightly soft.

2. Combine mushrooms, asparagus, spinach, risotto and cheese in a large bowl, blend well. Press the mixture into the peppers.

3. Pour the sherry vinegar in the bottom of a medium pot and heat on low heat. Put peppers in the sherry bath, open side up. Cover and simmer for 10-15 minutes.

Q2 Recommendation: Remove from heat, place on plate and drizzle with balsamic vinegar.

Makes 4 stuffed peppers.

Q2: 311 calories per pepper/serving, protein: 16.3g, carbohydrates: 33.7g, fat: 12.8g, fiber 2.1g

TEMPEH STIR FRY

- 8 oz. organic tempeh (packaged blend of brown rice, barley and millet)
- 1 T. olive oil
- 2 cups portobella mushrooms, sliced
- 1 cup bell peppers, tri-colored, sliced
- 1 cup asparagus, cut in 1-inch pieces
- ¾ cup edamame, steamed (or 1 cup sugar snap peas)
- 1 cup yellow onions, cut in 1-inch pieces
- ½ t. celery salt
- ½ t. garlic powder
- ½ t. ground black pepper
- 1 t. sesame oil
- 2-3 t. liquid aminos (substitute low-sodium soy sauce)

Optional: Sesame seeds

Q2 Tip: Cut up your favorite vegetables ahead of time for a super quick healthy meal. Add tempeh for a satisfying meatless meal, or if you prefer, tofu.

1. Steam the tempeh per directions on the package.
2. Place olive oil in a large skillet on medium-high heat for 1-2 minutes or until hot. Put vegetables, spices, sesame oil and amino acids in the skillet and stir fry for 3-5 minutes.
3. Add the tempeh and sesame seeds into the skillet and stir fry 2-3 minutes.

Q2 Recommendation: This is perfect to eat just like this. Wanting rice? Black rice or Creamy Lime Rice on page 211 pairs well with this stir fry.

Serves 4.

Q2: 261 calories per serving, protein: 19.4g, carbohydrates: 19.5g, fat: 14.3g, fiber 4.5g

SEAFOOD

Mesquite Salmon - Page 230

Seared Scallop Stacks - Page 233

Shrimp Scampi - Page 234

The Making of Fish Parcels - Page 227

COD FISH ROLLS

- 4 (5-6 ounce) pieces of cod, cut 1/3" thick
- 2 fresh lemons
- Handful of baby spinach
- Paprika, for garnish and flavor

2 T. of Spinach Artichoke Dip for each cod filet (recipe on page 158)

Q2 Tip: Use toothpicks or food twine to keep the fish rolls closed while cooking.

1. Place one cod filet on a plate and scoop 2 T. of the spinach artichoke dip lengthwise on the filet. Cover the dip with a thin layer of baby spinach leaves.

2. Roll the narrow end to the wide end of the filet. Carefully use food twine or secure with a toothpick. Place fish roll in a baking dish. Repeat with each roll.

3. Squeeze ½ lemon on each roll. Sprinkle each roll with paprika. Place in pre-heated oven.

Bake: 375 degrees for 15 minutes.

Serves 4.

Q2: 227 calories per serving, protein: 38.9g, carbohydrates: 7.3g, fat: 4.9g, fiber 1.3g

FISH PARCELS

- 1 5-6 oz. fish filet of your choice for each meal (parcel)
- Baby tri-colored potatoes; 3-4 split in half for each meal (parcel)
- Veggies of your choice, green beans, Brussels sprouts, broccoli, asparagus, etc.
- ½ Fresh lemon, juiced, for each fish parcel
- Fine-grain sea salt, to taste
- Ground black pepper, to taste
- Parchment paper, cut in 12x12 squares
- Aluminum foil, cut in 12x12 squares

Q2 Tip: Incorporate various spices in your parcels to your liking.

1. Place the fish in the middle of the parchment paper and pour juice of ½ lemon on top along with spices of your choice (See below).

2. Arrange potatoes and vegetables around the fish and dash with a little salt and paper.

3. Seal the parchment paper securely with a little space for expansion of steam, then wrap in aluminum foil in case of leakage. Place parcels on baking sheet.

Bake at 400 degrees for 12-15 minutes. Remove from oven and let rest for 5 minutes before opening. Be careful of the steam when opening.

Detox: Season with turmeric and/or cumin.

Fresh: Season with chives.

Greek: Season with oregano and fresh garlic.

Piccata: Season with capers and parsley.

Smoky: Season with smoked paprika.

Spicy: Season with crushed red pepper or cayenne pepper.

Italian: Season with oregano, fresh garlic and a splash of balsamic vinegar.

Serve 1 per parcel.

Q2: 259 calories per parcel/serving*, protein: 29.8g, carbohydrates: 33.4g, fat: 1.3g, fiber 7.9

The calculation will vary dependent on ingredients.
This calculation was with four potatoes and twelve green beans.

MISO GLAZED FISH (COD, SEA BASS, HALIBUT)

- 4 (5-6 ounce each) cod, sea bass or halibut Filets
- 1 T. bonita miso
- 1 T. seasoned rice vinegar
- ½ t. toasted sesame oil
- 1 t. liquid aminos (substitute low-sodium soy sauce)
- 1 green onion, chopped thin
- 1 T. sesame seeds
- Parchment Paper

Q2 Tip: Set the rack in the oven so that is 4 inches away from the heating element. Preheat the oven to 400 degrees. You can also marinate the fish overnight so that it is ready to prepare.

1. Whisk the miso, vinegar, sesame oil and liquid aminos in a small bowl.

2. Pour into a marinade dish or secured bag and place the fish filets in, coat completely. Let it sit for at least one hour.

3. Place a wire rack on top of a baking sheet. Remove the fish from the marinade, discarding the marinade, and place the fish on the rack and put into the oven.

Bake at 400 degrees for 12-15 minutes, until fish flakes off easily when tested with a fork.

Serves 4.

Q2: 218 calories per serving*, protein: 42.1g, carbohydrates: 2.2g, fat: 3.5g, fiber 0.6

*The calculation will vary dependent on selection of fish. This calculation was with sea bass.

MESQUITE SALMON

- 4 (5-6 ounces) salmon, wild caught or sockeye
- 1 t. smoked paprika
- ½ t. garlic powder
- ¼ t. onion salt
- ¼ t. cayenne pepper
- 1 fresh lemon

Q2 Tip: You can control the salt intake and strength of flavoring when you make your own flavors, like this mesquite flavoring.

1. Place filets on a slightly greased cooking pan.
2. Mix the paprika, garlic powder, onion salt and cayenne pepper in a bowl. Set aside.
3. Squeeze ¼ of the lemon on each filet and sprinkle ½ t. of the combined spices on each filet. Place in a pre-heated oven.

Bake: 400 degrees for 15 minutes.

Serves 4.

Q2: 288 calories per serving, protein: 39.5g, carbohydrates: 2g, fat: 12.7g, fiber 0.7g

SALMON VEGGIE BOWL

- Mesquite Salmon recipe on page 230
- ¾ cup of Creamy Lime Rice on page 211

Or

- ¾ cup Roasted Red Pepper Risotto on page 222
- ½ cup vegetables or beans of your choice, spinach, broccoli, black beans, etc.

Q2 Tip: Transform these recipes into a well-balanced meal.
1. Place rice or risotto in a bowl, top it off with salmon and steamed or sautéed vegetables, beans or other choices.

Q2 Favorite: Creamy Lime Rice with Salmon, black beans and Roasted Red Pepper Risotto with salmon, spinach and broccoli.

Makes 1 bowl* ~ using one serving of salmon and creamy lime rice plus ½ cup black beans.

Q2: 374 calories per serving*, protein: 41.3g, carbohydrates: 21.4g, fat: 4.2g, fiber 0.9g

The calculation will vary dependent on your selection. This calculation is based on the Q2 Favorite combination ~ ½ cup Creamy Lime Rice and ½ cup black beans.

SEARED SCALLOPS w/EDAMAME GINGER DRESSING

Sauce:

- 1 cup edamame, shelled
- 1 garlic clove, chopped
- 1 cup water
- 1 fresh lemon, juiced
- 2 T. extra-virgin olive oil
- 3 t. ginger root, chopped
- ½ t. fine-grain sea salt

Scallops:

- 1/3 cup shallots, chopped
- 2 T. grapeseed Oil
- 1 lb. sea scallops
- 2 T. butter
- Optional: ½ cup tomatoes, diced for garnish

Q2 Tip: Make the Edamame Ginger Dressing first as scallops take minimal time to cook.

1. In a medium saucepan, bring edamame, garlic and water to a boil. Reduce heat until edamame is tender, about five minutes. Transfer the mixture to a food processor. Add the lemon juice, olive oil, ginger root and sea salt. Blend until smooth. Transfer back to the saucepan and simmer on low for five minutes.

2. Pat the scallops dry to remove excess water. Heat oil in a large skillet, add shallots and then sea scallops. Make sure the scallops do not touch each other. Season scallops with salt and pepper and leave them untouched for three minutes. Gently flip scallops, add butter to pan and sear, about two minutes.

3. Remove scallops gently and place them on a serving dish. Spoon the dressing over each scallop. Finish with a diced tomato on each scallop before serving.

Serves 4.

Q2: 381 calories per serving, protein: 27.9g, carbohydrates: 13.8g, fat: 24.8g, fiber 3.1

Seared Scallop Stacks: Serve as an appetizer two different ways; spread edamame ginger dressing or Salsa Verde (on page 154) on a seeded tortilla chip round and stack with scallop and fresh tomato.

SHRIMP SCAMPI

- 1 lb. linguini (regular, quinoa or chickpea pasta)
- 2 cups reserved water from the cooked pasta
- 2 T. extra-virgin olive oil
- 1 large shallot, finely chopped
- 5 garlic cloves, finely chopped
- Pinch of red pepper flakes
- 24 medium-large shrimp, about 1 lb., cooked, peeled and deveined, tail on
- ½ cup dry white wine
- 2 fresh lemons, juiced
- 1/3 cup flat-leaf parsley, finely chopped

Q2 Tip: Start with step one and while the water is boiling, prepare step two. Don't forget to reserve two cups of water from the pasta when draining.

1. Bring a large pot of salted water to a boil to cook the pasta. Add the pasta and bring back to a boil, stirring so pasta does not stick. Cook two minutes less than the directions on the package. Drain the pasta BUT reserve 2 cups of the water.

2. In a large skillet, heat olive oil over medium heat. Sauté the shallots, garlic and red pepper flakes for one minute, then add the shrimp. Sauté the shrimp for two minutes, then flip for an additional two minutes. Remove shrimp from the pan; set aside and keep warm.

3. Add wine and lemon juice to the large skillet. Add butter until melted, then return the shrimp to the pan along with the

cooked pasta and reserved water for two minutes, stirring well. Remove from heat.

Q2 Finishing Touch: Toss with fresh parsley and serve with fresh parmesan cheese.

Serves 6.

Q2: 425 calories per serving*, protein: 39.1g, carbohydrates: 47.5g, fat: 10.9g, fiber 11.3

> *The calculation will vary dependent on your selection of pasta. This calculation is based on using chickpea pasta.

Salmon or Shrimp Stir Fry – Substitute salmon or shrimp for the Tempeh – Recipe on Page 224.

Add your pre-cooked salmon or shrimp to any salad in the Salad Section – Page 171.

CHICKEN

Balsamic Chicken - Page 240

Chicken Parcels - Page 238

Quick Chicken Salad - Page 244

Shepherd's Pie Remix - Page 245

Spicy Orange Chicken - Page 246

CHICKEN PARCELS

〰〰〰〰〰〰〰〰〰〰〰〰〰〰〰〰〰〰〰〰〰〰

- 1 boneless skinless chicken breast for each meal (parcel)
- Baby tri-colored potatoes
- Veggies of your choice: green beans, Brussels sprouts, broccoli, asparagus, etc.
- ½ fresh lemon, juiced, for each Chicken Parcel
- Fine-grain sea salt, to taste
- Ground black pepper, to taste
- Parchment paper, cut in 12x12 squares
- Aluminum foil, cut in 12x12 squares

Q2 Tip: Use a roll of parchment paper on one side and aluminum foil on the other side.

1. Place the chicken in the middle of the parchment paper and pour juice of ½ lemon on top along with spices of your choice (See below).

2. Arrange potatoes and vegetables around the chicken and dash with a little salt and paper.

3. Seal the parchment paper securely with a little space for expansion of steam then wrap in aluminum foil in case of leakage. Place parcels on baking sheet.

Bake at 400 degrees for 20-25 minutes. Remove from oven and let rest for 5 minutes before opening. Be careful of the steam when opening.

Detox: Season with turmeric and/or cumin.

Greek: Season with oregano and fresh garlic.

Piccata: Season with capers and parsley.

Smoky: Season with smoked paprika.

Spicy: Season with crushed red pepper or cayenne pepper.

Italian: Season with oregano, fresh garlic and a splash of balsamic vinegar.

Serve 1 per parcel.

Q2: 350 calories per parcel/serving* protein: 40.6g, carbohydrates: 39.9g, fat: 4.1g, fiber 6g

*The calculation will vary dependent on ingredients. This calculation was with three potatoes and four broccoli florets.

BALSAMIC CHICKEN (GRILL AND OVEN METHOD)

- 1 lb. boneless skinless chicken breasts
- ¼ cup grapeseed or olive oil
- ¼ cup balsamic vinegar
- 1 T. pure honey
- 2 garlic cloves, minced
- 2 T. rosemary, fresh preferred (substitute ground rosemary)
- 1 t. dried oregano
- ½ t. fine-grain sea salt
- ¼ t. ground black pepper

Q2 Tip: Marinate the chicken overnight if using grilling method.

1. Combine the avocado oil, balsamic vinegar, honey, garlic, rosemary, oregano, salt and pepper in a large bowl.
2. Glaze the chicken breasts with the marinade and grill over medium-high heat approximately 8-10 minutes per side – dependent on thickness of breasts.
3. OR lay the chicken, juices and marinade in a baking dish and put in the oven uncovered on the center rack.

Bake at 400 degrees for 25-30 minutes.

Serves 4.

Q2: 276 calories per serving, protein: 33.2g, carbohydrates: 11.3g, fat: 10.5g, fiber 1.5

CINNAMON CHICKEN W/APPLE CONFIT (GRILLED OR OVEN METHOD)

- 1 lb. boneless skinless chicken breasts
- 1/8 cup grapeseed or olive oil
- 1 T. ground cinnamon
- 1 t. ground turmeric
- ¼ t. cayenne pepper
- ½ t. fine-grain sea salt
- Apple Confit:

- 3 apples, cored, cut into small chunks with skin
- ¾ cup shallots, diced
- 1 T. pure honey
- 1 T. butter
- 1 T. sherry wine vinegar
- ¼ t. fine-grain sea salt
- ¼ t. ground black pepper

Q2 Tip: Marinate the chicken overnight if using grilling method.

1. Mix the oil, cinnamon, turmeric, cayenne pepper and salt in a bowl.

2. Place the marinated chicken breasts on a grill over medium-high heat approximately 8-10 minutes per side – dependent on thickness of breasts OR lay the chicken, juices and marinade in a baking dish and put in oven uncovered on the center rack.

3. Bring apples, shallots, honey, butter, vinegar, salt and pepper to a simmer in a medium saucepan over medium-low heat. Cook until tender, about 10 minutes. Add sherry wine vinegar and remove from the heat.

Bake at 400 degrees for 25-30 minutes. To serve, spoon apples and shallots over each chicken breast.

Serves 4.

Q2: 448 calories per serving, protein: 34.2g, carbohydrates: 40.5g, fat: 18g, fiber 5.1

MISO GLAZED CHICKEN (GRILL AND OVEN METHOD)

- 1 lb. boneless skinless chicken breasts
- 1 T. bonita miso
- 1 T. seasoned rice vinegar
- 1 t. liquid aminos (you can substitute low-sodium soy sauce)
- ½ t. toasted sesame oil
- 1 green onion, chopped thinly
- Sesame seeds

Q2 Tip: Marinate the chicken overnight if using grilling method.

1. Mix the miso, rice vinegar, liquid aminos and sesame oil in a bowl.
2. Place the marinated chicken breasts on a grill over medium-high heat approximately 8-10 minutes per side, dependent on thickness of breasts.
3. OR lay the chicken, juices and marinade in a baking dish and put in oven uncovered on the center rack.

Bake at 400 degrees for 25-30 minutes. Remove from heat then serve with green onions and sesame seeds.

Serves 4.

Q2: 244 calories per serving, protein: 33.9g, carbohydrates: 2.2g, fat: 10.4g, fiber 0.6g

MISO CHICKEN LETTUCE WRAPS

- 1 recipe of the cooked marinated Miso Glazed Chicken (page 242)
- 1 recipe of the marinade for the Miso Glazed Chicken (page 242)
- Lettuce wraps
- Shredded cabbage, carrots and chicory

Q2 Tip: Add various other toppings; slivered almonds, slivered peppers, bean sprouts or rice noodles.

One Step: Arrange chicken with extra sauce in the middle of the wrap length-wise along with topping of your choice. Fold each end of the lettuce wrap to serve or enjoy.

Makes 16 Lettuce Wraps

Q2: 61 calories per wrap/serving*, protein: 8.5g, carbohydrates: 0.6g, fat: 2.6g, fiber 0.2

Calculation is without the toppings.

Miso Chicken Lettuce Wraps

QUICK CHICKEN SALAD

) 1 lb. chicken, cooked – cubed or shredded

) ½ cup plain Greek yogurt, 0%

) ½ cup celery, sliced

) ½ cup red grapes, cut in half

) ½ cup walnuts or almonds, chopped

) ½ t. celery salt

) ½ t. paprika

) ¼ t. ground black pepper

Q2 Tip: Eat plain, spoon into a tomato or large pepper, or in a lettuce or multi-grain wrap.

One Step: Mix all ingredients in a bowl. Enjoy or fill in your choice of vegetable or bread.

For best results, refrigerate for at least one hour before serving.

Serves 6

Q2: 241 calories per serving, protein: 34.5g, carbohydrates: 7.5g, fat: 8.5g, fiber 0.9

SHEPHERD'S PIE REMIX

- 1 lb. boneless skinless chicken breasts, cooked – cubed or shredded
- 2 large baked sweet potatoes
- 2 cups various vegetables; zucchini, squash, carrots, onions, etc.
- Fine-grain sea salt, to taste
- Ground black pepper, to taste

Q2 Tip: This is especially easy to prepare if you prepare for the week and have these ingredients pre-made and ready to use. Use the parchment paper method to cook your chicken (See Chicken Parcels – Page 238). Bake whole sweet potatoes in the oven for the week so that they are ready to eat, accompany a meal or to combine in a casserole.

1. Steam the veggies until they are slightly softened. Season to taste with salt and pepper.

2. Place the chicken in a ramekin, put veggies on top and cap it off with a scoop of sweet potato. Ramekins are ready to eat OR store in the refrigerator for the week.

3. To serve as a casserole; layer the chicken, veggies and sweet potatoes in a baking dish. For larger portion, double the recipe. Once in the casserole, place in the oven.

Bake at 350 degrees for 15 minutes.

Serves 6.

Q2 Variation: Use cauliflower, tempeh, turkey, pork or beef in place of chicken.

Q2: 206 calories per ramekin/serving, protein: 23.3g, carbohydrates: 14.6g, fat: 5.7g, fiber 0.6g

SPICY ORANGE CHICKEN (GRILL AND OVEN METHOD)

- 1 lb. boneless skinless chicken breasts
- 2-3 oranges, juiced (approximately 1/3 cup)
- 2 t. smoked paprika
- 1 t. ground chipotle chili pepper
- 1 t. ground coriander
- 1 t. ground cumin
- 1 t. garlic powder
- 1 t. onion powder
- 1 t. Mexican oregano (substitute ground oregano)
- 1 t. ground black pepper
- ½ t. ground cayenne pepper
- ½ t. fine-grain sea salt

Q2 Tip: Marinate the chicken overnight if using grilling method.

1. Mix the orange juice, paprika, chili pepper, coriander, cumin, garlic, onion, oregano, black pepper, cayenne pepper and salt in a bowl.
2. Place the marinated chicken breasts on a grill over medium-high heat approximately 8-10 minutes per side – dependent on thickness of breasts.
3. OR lay the chicken, juices and marinade in a baking dish and put in oven uncovered on the center rack.

Bake at 400 degrees for 25-30 minutes.

Serves 4.

Q2: 271 calories per serving, protein: 34.2g, carbohydrates: 13.2g, fat: 8.9g, fiber 3.1g

Chicken Scampi – Substitute Chicken for the Shrimp – Recipe on Page 234.

Chicken Stir Fry - Add Chicken or substitute for the Tempeh – Recipe on Page 224.

Add your pre-cooked favorite Chicken to any salad in the Salad Section – Page 171.

PORK & BEEF

Spicy Crock Pot Pork - Page 248

Stuffed Pork Chops with Goat Cheese - Page 249

Braciole - Page 250

SPICY CROCK POT PORK

- 2 lbs. pork tenderloin
- 1 cup vegetable stock, organic – zero to low-sodium
- 2 T. apple cider vinegar
- 4 garlic cloves, minced
- 1 serrano pepper, seeded and minced (omit for less spicy)
- 1 t. ground cumin
- 1 t. ground turmeric
- ½ t. fine-grain sea salt
- ½ t. ground black pepper

Q2 Tip: Add carrots, potatoes, Brussels sprouts or other vegetables in the crock pot for a well-rounded one pot meal.

1. Place one cup of vegetable stock in a crock pot. Mix the vinegar, garlic, serrano pepper, cumin, turmeric, salt and pepper in a bowl.

2. Glaze the pork tenderloin with the marinade and place in the slow cooker. Pour the rest of the marinade on top of the tenderloin. Place vegetables of your choice around the tenderloin and season with a little salt and pepper.

3. Slow cook on low setting for 8 hours.

Serves 8.

Q2: 174 calories per serving, protein: 30.3g, carbohydrates: 1.9g, fat: 4.2g, fiber 0.7g

STUFFED PORK CHOPS W/ GOAT CHEESE

- 4 pork chops, thick cut
- 2 T. olive oil
- 1 cup bread crumbs, freshly made preferred
- 1 cup vegetable stock, organic – zero to low-sodium
- 6 oz. goat cheese, crumbled (You can substitute with another cheese, if you wish)
- ½ t. fine-grain sea salt
- ½ t. black pepper
- ½ t. garlic powder

Q2 Tip: The Slow Cooked Apple Quinoa Porridge on Page 141 is a nice complement along with fresh green beans or grilled asparagus.

1. Marinate the pork chops overnight in 2 T. olive oil with salt, pepper and garlic powder.

2. Cut pork chops lengthwise to butterfly, keeping an opening so that you can stuff them. In a separate bowl, mix the bread crumbs and crumbled goat cheese.

3. Spoon bread crumb mixture into each chop, then place pork chops in a heated, slightly oiled pan and brown on each side. Transfer the chops to a baking dish and pour the vegetable stock on top. Cover and place in a pre-heated oven.

Bake at 375 degrees for 40 minutes. Let the pork chops sit at room temperature for three minutes before serving to enhance the juices, flavor and texture.

Serves 4.

Q2: 445 calories per serving, protein: 30g, carbohydrates: 21.6g, fat: 27.6g, fiber 2.1g

Pork Stir Fry - Add Pork or substitute for the Tempeh – Recipe on Page 245.

Shepherd's Pie Remix – Use Spicy Slow Cooker Pork (Page 248) in place of Chicken – Recipe on Page 245.

BRACIOLE

- 1 lb. flank steak, sliced into 8 thin slices
- 1 cup bread crumbs, freshly made preferred or 1 cup gluten-free panko
- 8 oz. fresh parmesan cheese, grated
- 4 garlic cloves, minced
- ½ t. fine-grain sea salt
- ½ t. black pepper
- 1/2 cup beef stock, organic - unsalted

Q2 Tip: Serve with cooked juices or with Simple Marinara on Page 200. Pairs well with steamed broccoli, asparagus or green beans.

1. Mix the bread crumbs, parmesan cheese, garlic, salt and pepper in a small bowl.

2. Lay out the thin steak slice and place 2 T. of the bread crumb mixture lengthwise. Then roll the meat the same way from the short end first. Tie with cooking string on each side to secure the contents. Repeat with each steak.

3. Place each rolled steak (end side down) in a heated, slightly oiled pan and brown on each side. Transfer the rolled steaks to a baking dish and pour the vegetable stock on top. Cover and place in a pre-heated oven.

Bake at 375 degrees for 20 minutes. If using the Simple Marinara to dress with, then drain the liquid and pour marinara over the braciole.

Q2 Favorite: Serve over cannellini beans and lentils in the simple marinara sauce.

Makes 8 bracioles.

Q2: 216 calories per braciole/serving, protein: 25.5g, carbohydrates: 3.8g, fat: 10.9g, fiber 0.2g

SLOW COOKED BARBACOA

- 3 lb. chuck roast, grass-fed
- 1 cup beef stock, organic - unsalted
- 2 T. apple cider vinegar
- 1 small yellow onion, minced
- 4 garlic cloves, minced
- 1 serrano pepper, seeded and minced
- 1 T. ground cumin
- ¼ t. ground cloves
- 1 t. fine-grain sea salt
- 3 bay leaves
- 1 Fresh Lime, juiced, plus additional lime wedges to serve with

Q2 Tip: Serve with Cauliflower Creamy Rice on page 211 or make it a wrap with homemade guacamole and Salsa Verde on page 154.

1. Place one cup of beef stock in a slow cooker. Mix the vinegar, onion, garlic, serrano pepper, cumin, cloves, salt and bay leaves in a bowl.

2. Glaze the chuck roast with the marinade and place in the slow cooker. Pour the rest of the marinade on top of the roast.

3. Slow cook on low setting for 8 hours. Remove meat with some of the juices and squeeze one lime on the meat. Serve with additional lime wedges and vegetables and condiments of your choice.

Serves 12.

Q2: 255 calories per serving, protein: 37.9g, carbohydrates: 1.9g, fat: 9.6g, fiber 0.4g

Beef Stir Fry - Add beef or substitute for the tempeh – Recipe on Page 224.

Shepherd's Pie Remix – Use Slow Cooked Barbacoa (above) or lean grass-fed ground beef in place of chicken – Recipe on Page 245.

DESSERTS

Key Lime Shooters - Page 260

Chia Pudding with Fresh
Berries - Page 256

Sweet Potato Nice Cream - Page 263

Chocolate Avocado Pudding, page 257
Chocolate Beet Cake, page 258

APPLE TART

Crust:

- 1 cup almond flour
- 1 cup walnuts
- 1 egg
- 1 T. coconut oil

Filling:

- 2 T. pure maple syrup
- 8 oz. coconut milk, 100% - unsweetened
- 1 egg
- 3 egg yolks
- ¼ cup pure maple syrup
- 3 large red apples

Optional: 1 lemon

Q2 Tip: Slice your apples right before you are ready to use or squeeze lemon on them until you are ready to use to keep them from oxidizing (turning brown).

1. Combine almond flour, walnuts, 1 egg, coconut oil and 2 T. maple syrup in a food processor and process until a smooth dough forms.

2. Spread the dough into an 8-inch round tart or quiche pan. Start from the center of the pan and gently push with your fingers until the bottom and the sides are completely covered. Layer the apples evenly on the crust.

3. Whisk coconut milk, egg, egg yolks, and maple syrup until blended thoroughly. Spread the slightly thickened mixture on top of the apples.

Bake: 350 degrees for 35-40 minutes or until the crust and apples start browning.

Serves 8.

Q2: 258 calories per serving, protein: 7.7g, carbohydrates: 24.1g, fat: 16.6g, fiber 3.5g

BAKED PEARS WITH WALNUTS AND HONEY

- 2 large ripe pears
- Ground cinnamon
- Honey
- Walnuts, or nuts of your choice

Q2 Tip: When you are craving something sweet, grab your favorite fruit and transform it like in this Q2 Favorite recipe.

1. Cut the pears in half and scoop out the seeds using a spoon or melon baller.
2. Place on a baking pan and sprinkle with desired amount of cinnamon, honey and walnuts.

Bake: 350 degrees for 30 minutes

Serves 4.

Q2: 110 calories per serving*, protein: 2.1g, carbohydrates: 18.1g, fat: 4.3g, fiber 3.7g

*Calculated by one half of pear, 1 t. honey, 1-ounce walnuts with a sprinkle of cinnamon.

CHIA PUDDING

- 16 oz. coconut milk, 100% - unsweetened
- ¼ cup chia seeds
- 1 ½ t. pure vanilla extract
- 1 t. ground cinnamon
- 1 t. ground nutmeg
- ½ t. ground ginger
- 1-2 T. agave nectar, pure honey or pure maple syrup, to your desired sweetness and flavor
- Fresh berries, pomegranates, or other fruit and toppings

Q2 Tip: Keep this delightful treat in your refrigerator so that you can create your own chia bowl at your convenience.

1. Whisk the coconut milk, chia seeds, vanilla, cinnamon, nutmeg, ginger and sweetener in a bowl. Refrigerate for one hour.
2. Remove from the refrigerator and whisk thoroughly to keep the chia seeds from clumping and settling to the bottom.
3. Refrigerate for at least two more hours.

Ready to enjoy plain. Spoon your favorite berries on top or other fruit and garnishes.

Q2 Favorite: Topped with mixed berries, unsweetened coconut flakes, cacao nibs and slivered almonds.

Serves 4.

Q2: 80 calories per serving plain, protein: 1.7g, carbohydrates: 8.9g, fat: 4.4g, fiber 2.9g

CHOCOLATE AVOCADO PUDDING

- 3 large ripe avocados, peeled, pitted and quartered
- 1/3 cup cocoa powder, unsweetened
- 1/3 cup agave nectar
- ½ cup coconut milk, 100% - unsweetened
- 2 t. pure vanilla
- 1 or 2 pinches of cinnamon, to your liking

Q2 Tip: Make it spicy chocolate pudding and add 1/8 t. Cayenne Pepper.

1. Blend avocados, cocoa powder, agave nectar, coconut milk, vanilla extract, and cinnamon in a blender or food processor.
2. Taste and add a little more agave nectar if you wish a sweeter taste or cinnamon.
3. Refrigerate pudding until chilled, about an hour or two.

Q2 Recommendation: Serve shooter-style, layered with Granola (page 140) and top with a banana slice or berry. Makes 12-16.

Serves 8.

Q2: 180 calories per serving, protein: 2.3g, carbohydrates: 15.5g, fat: 14.1g, fiber 6.4g

CHOCOLATE BEET CAKE

- Coconut oil, to grease baking pan
- Cocoa powder, unsweetened, to dust baking pan
- 1 ½ cups almond flour (you can substitute brown rice flour or other)
- ½ cup cocoa powder, unsweetened
- 1 ½ t. baking powder
- 1 t. cinnamon
- 1 t. fine-grain sea salt
- 4 large eggs
- ½ cup coconut oil
- 1/3 cup pure honey
- ¼ cup almond or coconut sugar (dependent on flavor that you desire)
- 1 ½ t. pure vanilla
- 1 lb. beets, cooked (approximately 4 pre-packaged cooked beets)

Optional: Chocolate Avocado Pudding recipe for frosting

Q2 Tip: Make the chocolate avocado pudding on page 257 ahead of time so that you can frost the top of this cake to make it a double -chocolate delicacy, delicious and nutritious. Want to make cupcakes? No problem. Simply use cupcake liners and bake for 25-30 minutes. Yields 24 cupcakes.

1. Grease one 9-inch round cake pan with a little coconut oil and line the bottom with parchment paper. Slightly oil the parchment paper and dust the pan with cocoa powder.

Set aside. Combine the dry ingredients; flour, cocoa powder, baking powder, cinnamon and salt. Set aside.

2. Blend coconut oil, honey and sugar in a large bowl with an electric mixer for 2 minutes then beat in one egg at a time. Add vanilla and beets and blend for 3 minutes. Gradually add the flour mixture and beat until thoroughly blended.

3. Pour the batter into the prepared pan. Bake on the middle rack.

Bake: 350 degrees for 45-50 minutes or until the cake springs back when slightly touched.

Let cool completely before transferring to a serving dish. Frost the top of the cake with Avocado Chocolate Pudding. Double chocolate, nutritious and delicious!

Serves 10 per cake. Makes 20 cupcakes.

Q2: 225 calories per cake serving*, protein: 5g, carbohydrates: 21.8g, fat: 15.6g, fiber 2.8g

113 calories per cupcake/serving*, protein: 2.5g, carbohydrates: 10.9g, fat: 7.8g, fiber 1.4g

*Calculated plain – without frosting.

KEY LIME SHOOTERS

- 4 key limes, juiced
- 2 ripe avocados, peeled, pitted and quartered
- ¼ cup agave nectar
- Optional: Granola, nuts or another crunch factor, 2 t. per shooter
- Raspberry for topping

Q2 Tip: Use key limes for best results, however, limes can be used.

1. Blend avocados, lime and agave nectar in a blender or food processor.
2. Taste and add a little more agave nectar if you wish a sweeter taste.
3. Refrigerate pudding until chilled, about an hour or two.

Q2 Recommendation: Serve shooter-style layered with Granola (page and top with raspberry.

Makes 6 shooters without granola or nuts. Makes 12 shooters with two layers of granola.

Q2: 75 calories per serving plain, protein: 0.7g, carbohydrates: 10.2g, fat: 4.5g, fiber 2.9g

With 1 T. Granola:178 calories/serving, protein: 3.5g, carbohydrates: 17.9g, fat: 11.7g, fiber 4.8g

PUMPKIN PARFAITS

〰〰〰〰〰〰〰〰〰〰〰〰〰〰〰〰〰〰〰〰〰〰〰

- 1 lb. ricotta cheese, fresh
- 1 15-oz. can pumpkin
- ¼ cup pure maple syrup

Optional for topping: Pecans, walnuts, almonds, coconut, cinnamon

Q2 Tip: Refrigerate for at least one hour before serving.

One Step: Combine ricotta, pumpkin and maple syrup. Scoop ½ cup in serving dishes and serve or top with your favorite topping(s).

Serves 6.

Q2: 163 calories per serving, protein: 9.4g, carbohydrates: 18.4g, fat: 6.2g, fiber 2.1g

Pumpkin Parfaits

TWICE AS NICE ICE CREAM

- Chocolate Strawberry Nice Cream
- 6 bananas, frozen and cut into slices
- 6 T. cocoa powder, unsweetened
- 1 cup frozen strawberries
- ¼ cup heavy cream

Q2 Tip: Cut bananas in slices and freeze until ready to use.

One Step: Blend the bananas, cocoa powder, strawberries and heavy cream in a high-performance blender or food processor until smooth and creamy. Remove and serve immediately for a soft-serve texture or freeze until ready to eat or let it set in the freezer for at least 8 hours for a harder consistency.

Q2 Recommendation: Run an ice cream scoop under warm water when you are ready to scoop out the ice cream from the freezer.

Serves 6.

Q2: 143 calories per serving, protein: 2.4g, carbohydrates: 32.2g, fat: 3g, fiber 5.2g

SWEET POTATO NICE CREAM

- 2 lbs. sweet potatoes, baked
- 1 banana, frozen and cut into slices
- Juice from the baked sweet potatoes
- ½ cup pure honey
- ¼ cup heavy cream
- 1 t. cinnamon
- ½ t. nutmeg

Q2 Tip: Include the juices of the baked sweet potatoes for ultimate flavor. Store in the freezer in a freezer-approved container.

1. Peel the cooled sweet potatoes.
2. Blend the sweet potatoes, honey, heavy cream, cinnamon and nutmeg in a food processor or a high-performance blender until smooth and creamy.
3. Place in the freezer for at least 8 hours before serving.

Serves 6.

Q2: 268 calories per serving, protein: 1.8g, carbohydrates: 62.4g, fat: 2g, fiber 5.2g

UPSIDE DOWN RICOTTA DESSERT

- 1 lb. ricotta cheese, fresh
- 2 T. pure honey
- 2 to 3 drops of pure vanilla or pure almond extract
- 1 T. lemon zest
- Fresh Berries of your choice, or other fruit

Q2 Tip: Keep this delightful treat in your refrigerator so that you can create your own upside- down ricotta dessert in seconds.

1. Blend ricotta cheese, honey, lemon zest, and extract in a blender or food processor – until smooth.
2. Refrigerate for at least one hour, then spoon over berries.

Serves 6.

Q2: 130 calories per serving, protein: 8.8g, carbohydrates: 11g, fat: 6.1g, fiber 0.7g

CONCLUSION

ove forward on your life's journey of change, healing and transformation. After all, change is the spice of life. Negative feelings and energy is detrimental to one's mental and physical health. Surround yourself with positive people, positive energy and positive self-talk. One thing that we did not talk about was the scale. Yes, that dreaded 'S' word. Well, the scale does not lie, but keep in mind that your daily nutritional intake and movement do not lie either. The scale can be a negative to those that are doing everything right and not seeing the results that they want to see – in turn, it can cause you to give up and slide back into your old habits. The scale can also be a positive, a way to remind yourself to keep trying, improving and changing. In either case, focus on your energy and overall well-being. Take notice of how your clothes feel as opposed to the numbers on the scale. It all begins in the mind, your perception, or how you look at things. Make it a goal to look at the glass half full, not half empty. Your mind can constantly play tricks on you, but you can be stronger and pursue your goal.

Transformation is a process – be patient and kind to yourself. Continue to improve your eating habits, move your body, allow mind time and embrace your life. Keep your why forefront. Prepare. Eat colorful. Seek balance in your life. Breathe. Find the happiness within yourself and about yourself. Be your own kind of beautiful. Share with others.

Final words, and how I end my mind-body practices of Yoga and Pilates ~ Close your eyes. Place your hands in prayer. As you lengthen your arms overhead to reawaken the physical body, push away any negative thoughts, energy or feelings, far, far away (as you push your arms down and behind you), always resist the negative and as you place your hands back together in prayer, restore the positive back within the mind, body and spirit. Keep the union with you for days and weeks to come. Bring it in to your day and into your tomorrow. Namaste.

Quotes and Thoughts to Live By

Inspirational and motivational quotes can impact the way that you think and the way that you live. They are gentle reminders to encourage you to do the right thing, stay on your life path and never give up until you have reached your goal, your dream, your prize. These are some of my favorite quotes that I used throughout this book, that I apply to my life and encourage others to do so also. Keep the following quotes forefront in your mind to help you stay on track.

- You Can Do It!
- Kick your bad habits by recognizing and changing your routine.
- Reach your goals with positive steps toward permanent changes with realistic expectations.
- Focus on the person that you are today so that you can be the person that you want to be tomorrow.
- Change your efforts to realistic solutions!
- Work on your weaknesses and fuel your strengths.
- Keep an open mind.

- Let go of past experiences!
- Get out of your own way!
- You can't cheat with bad eating and expect positive results.
- Fruits are nature's gift – fuel your body with fruits and balance out the natural sugar with lean protein.
- Attract balance in your life so that you can reach your goals with realistic expectations.
- Incorporate gut-health functional foods into your daily nutrition for a healthier you.
- Eat a rainbow every day for optimal health and overall well-being.
- Our bodies were meant to move, not to keep still.
- Add some flexibility in your life and create a positive effect on your workouts, everyday chores, your overall health and quality of life.
- "You can't expect to prevent negative feeling altogether. And you can't expect to experience positive feelings all the time. The Law of Emotional Choice directs us to acknowledge our feelings, but also to refuse to get stuck in the negative ones." -Greg Anderson
- "If you fail to plan, then you plan to fail." – Harvey MacKay
- "A goal without action is just a dream." – Dave Ramsey

If it roams on the land freely, if it swims in the sea ~
  If it grows on the Earth or if you can pick it off a tree.
And when you eat, quantity matters ~
  Share the knowledge in your chatters.
Make it matter, shut out the strife ~
  For this is A Recipe for a Healthy Life.
                    – Donna Fatigato

This simple verse I have used with my clients as a reminder of what and how to fuel their body and mind. It is a simple formula to live by. Don't make it hard. Create positivity in your life so that you can be the best version of yourself and live life to the fullest.

INDEX

About the Author

Donna Fatigato is an ACE-Certified Personal Trainer, Holistic Nutrition Coach, Group Fitness Instructor with specialties in Yoga, Pilates, Kickboxing and Spin. She has been in the fitness industry for over 30 years and the owner of Younique Lifelong Fitness, Inc., in Carol Stream, Illinois. There she has established accounts with various schools and businesses to keep the teachers and employees healthy. She teaches a monthly healthy cooking class in her MyHomeKitchen, also in Carol Stream. Donna is a professional member of the National Fitness Hall of Fame. Her articles have appeared in local newsletters.

You can learn more at www.youniquelifelongfitness.com.

Made in the USA
Lexington, KY
24 July 2018